D0456892

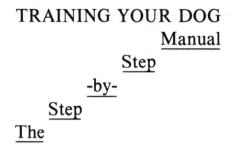

TRAINING YOUR DOG

Manual

Step

-by-

Step

The

A book for anyone who likes his dog
or who would like to like his dog.

To the memory of our dear friend

OLIVE POINT

Sept. 5, 1920 - Feb. 8, 1980

TRAINING YOUR DOG

The Step-by-Step Manual

by JOACHIM VOLHARD
and GAIL TAMASES FISHER

Drawings by Melissa Bartlett

Photographs by Roger Greenwald

FIRST EDITION

HOWELL BOOK HOUSE
New York

Copyright © 1983 by Howell Book House

All rights reserved. No part of this book may be reproduced or transmitted in any form or by any means, electronic or mechanical, including photocopying, recording or by any information storage and retrieval system, without permission in writing from the Publisher.

HOWELL BOOK HOUSE
Macmillan Publishing Company
866 Third Avenue, New York, NY 10022
Collier Macmillan Canada, Inc.

Library of Congress Cataloging in Publication Data

Volhard, Joachim.
    Training Your Dog.

    Bibliography: p. 234
    Includes index.
    1. Dogs—Training. 2. Dogs—Behavior. I. Fisher,
Gail Tamases. II. Title.
SF431.V64 1983   636.7′083   82-21327
ISBN 0-87605-775-X

Macmillan books are available at special discounts for bulk purchases for sales promotions, premiums, fund-raising, or educational use. For details, contact:

Special Sales Director
Macmillan Publishing Company
866 Third Avenue
New York, NY 10022

20   19   18   17

Printed in the United States of America

Contents

Feeding and Exercise / Vocabulary / Leash Training / Equipment / Long Line / Dumbbell / Whistle / The Collar / The Leash / How the Collar Works / How to Measure for a Collar / Extremes of Sensitivity / How to Hold the Leash / Handler Adaptations / How to Follow the Lessons / Anatomy of the Dog

About The Authors

JOACHIM ("JACK") VOLHARD is an internationally known dog obedience instructor. Since 1972 he has given obedience clinics all over America, Canada and England. He has authored numerous articles for various dog publications, including *Pure-bred Dogs, The American Kennel Gazette,* and he is the recipient of four awards from the Dog Writers' Association of America. His film *Puppy Aptitude Testing* was named Best Film on Dogs for 1980 by the DWAA.

In 1970 Jack met the late Olive S. Point of Richmond, Virginia. During their ten-year association they developed and perfected their instructional approach to training.

Jack and his wife, Wendy, breed, train and exhibit Landseer Newfoundlands. Jack has owned and trained many breeds including a Welsh Terrier, a German Shepherd Dog, a Collie, an English Springer Spaniel, a Yorkshire Terrier and a mixed breed.

Dog training is a hobby with Jack which he combines with a busy schedule as an Administrative Law Judge for the Department of Health and Human Services.

GAIL TAMASES FISHER has been training dogs professionally and teaching dog obedience classes for 12 years. In addition to running her own classes, Gail developed and instructed a 2-year college program teaching others to be obedience class instructors. She also taught a college course for dog breeders.

Gail has written many articles for dog publications including *Off-Lead*, the obedience training magazine, and *Pure-bred Dogs—American Kennel Gazette,* the American Kennel Club's official publication. She has conducted weekly pet columns in *The Manchester (N.H.) Union Leader* and *The Goffstown News.* She has also given many lectures and seminars on dog behavior, training and instructing, both in America and abroad.

Gail and her husband, Howard, raise Mastiffs and Vizslas which they train and show in both conformation and obedience.

JOACHIM VOLHARD   GAIL TAMASES FISHER

Foreword

WHAT MAKES this book so good? There are three major reasons. (1) Training methods are based on well-established psychological principles and are adapted to the mind of the dog. (2) Procedures are described in clear detail, with explicit criteria for going on to the next step of the training program. (3) Information is provided on how to select a dog to fit one's life style, and the importance of beginning training at the proper age. Other good features are recommendations for housing and feeding, and for the selection of equipment.

Common problems of dog behavior are illustrated by entertaining accounts of the misadventures of Konrad and other dogs. These should be useful to owners who often do not realize that their efforts to eliminate undesirable behavior actually reinforce it. Practical advice on even one behavioral problem could be worth the cost of the book.

Do I have any disagreements with the authors? None of consequence. They might have pointed out that there are important temperamental differences within as well as between breeds. Not all German Shepherds can be trained as guide dogs for the blind. The section on critical periods is excellent, but one need not give up hope if a dog's experiences do not fit the ideal pattern.

Jack Volhard and Gail Fisher are exceptionally good dog obedience instructors who have communicated their skills to many students. In this book they make their ideas and methods available to anyone for a modest investment in money, and a more substantial investment in time and effort. There is no magical way to train a dog to become a well-behaved member of human society. Those who are unwilling to make a substantial personal investment should not own a dog.

My final judgment. There are other good dog training books, but this may be the best yet.

JOHN L. FULLER

Author of numerous papers on learning and behavioral development in dogs and co-author of **Genetics and the Social Behavior of the Dog.** *From 1947 until 1970 Dr. Fuller worked at the Roscoe B. Jackson Laboratory in Bar Harbor, Maine, where he collaborated with Clarence Pfaffenberger of Guide Dogs for the Blind. From 1970 until 1978 he was Professor of Biopsychology at the State University of New York at Binghamton.*

Introduction

For NEARLY TWO DECADES, we have instructed people like you on an almost daily basis, how to successfully train their dogs. From the very beginning, we quickly discovered that knowing how to train a dog bears little, if any, relation to being a good instructor. An experienced trainer can make everything look easy, but this is of no help to someone just starting out.

The approach to training described in this book differs radically from other dog training methods. It is not based on personal aptitude, preference, or speculation. Instead, it rests on scientific research on canine behavior and learning and a thorough understanding of how people learn a new skill. This foundation provided the impetus for our step-by-step approach to training.

Our goal, in writing this book, is to provide the reader, the student of dog training, with a manual for the successful training of his dog. Lack of success leads to frustration and even anger. In many cases, the owner's disappointment reaches the stage where the dog is taken on a one-way trip to the pound. Success in training is the key to a mutually enjoyable relationship between owner and dog.

Uppermost in our minds is the belief that dog training should be fun for both the trainer and the dog. We hope that our book motivates you to motivate your dog.

Joachim J. Volhard
Gail Tamases Fisher

Acknowledgments

MOST AUTHORS begin an acknowledgment by thanking a spouse. We are no different. Wendy's and Howard's contributions in terms of patience, suggestions, support and understanding, not to mention the time spent haggling over a word, are immeasurable. The book would not have been possible without them.

Our students have been a constant source of encouragement, if not inspiration, for this work. It is they who continuously remind us of the need for improvement and growth. To those who have asked us over the years when this book would be written, here it is.

Our special thanks to those students and their dogs who volunteered their time for the photograph session: Connie Draper, Joan Greenwald, Elaine Lehr, Eric Louis, Garian Ovitt, Steve Youngentob, and the photographer, Roger Greenwald.

Jocelyn Hartley and Su-Ann Brown, who are also obedience instructors, reviewed the manuscript and we are grateful for their suggestions.

Melissa Bartlett has been doing the drawings for a number of our articles. Her contribution to this book will enhance not only your understanding, but your enjoyment as well. For this, we are grateful.

It is every author's dream to find a proofreader who understands grammar, has a sharp eye, and is in tune with the subject matter. We consider ourselves extremely fortunate in having had such an individual help us with this difficult task. Our sincere thanks to Alexandra Fisher.

For his encouragement and guidance, special thanks to Brother Job of the Monks of New Skete.

This book would not have been written without the enthusiasm, dedication and innovation of Olive Point. It was Olive's strong belief in the importance of understanding not only sound principles of dog training, but also the mechanics of teaching people, that laid the foundation for this step-by-step approach to dog training. It was her zeal, foresight and inspiration that brought us together in this labor of love.

Anyone who cannot live with a terrier's digging should not have a terrier.

Dogs are social creatures who enjoy our company as much as we enjoy theirs. . .and in general mirror our moods.

1

The Mind
of the Dog

DOG TRAINING is a term used to describe two different activities: (1) to teach a dog to do something he would not do on his own, and (2) to inhibit him from activities he would do on his own, but which we consider objectionable. In both instances we have to recognize the dog's limitations. We cannot train a dog to read and it would be useless to try, just as we cannot modify certain behavior no matter how objectionable we might consider it.

Anyone who finds the male dog's lifting of his leg objectionable should not have a male dog. Anyone who cannot live with a terrier's digging should not have a terrier. While some canine behaviors can be modified, it would be cruel even to attempt to change others. The moral is: understand your dog and let him *be* a dog.

In this chapter we will describe in detail what you can and cannot expect from man's best friend. First, we will discuss specific influences which either enhance or inhibit and, in some instances, impede learning. Second, we will deal with the limitations of the dog's mental abilities. Third, we will explain how the dog is able to learn what we want him to know.

CRITICAL PERIODS

A critical period is a specific time in a dog's life when an apparently insignificant experience may and often does have a great effect on later behavior. All dogs, regardless of breed or mix, are affected in their psychological growth by their environment. Critical periods apply to all dogs, but not necessarily to the same degree. Understanding these critical periods helps you to understand your dog's behavior and to know how to handle both him and yourself during certain special times.

Birth to Seven Weeks (0-49 Days)

In order to maximize the mental and psychological development of a puppy, it is absolutely essential that he remain in the nest with his mother and littermates until seven weeks of age. It is during this time that puppies learn that they are dogs. While playing, they practice different body postures, learning what they mean and what effects they have on brothers, sisters and mother. They learn what it feels like to bite and be bitten and what barking sounds like. Such activity tempers their own biting and barking.

Puppies are disciplined by Mom in a way they clearly understand. They learn to be submissive to her leadership, which teaches them to accept discipline. If a pup has not learned to accept leadership in its early dog-to-dog interactions, its training will be more difficult.

Puppies that are removed from the nest too early tend to be nervous, prone to barking and biting, and less responsive to discipline. Often they are more aggressive with other dogs. In general, a puppy taken away to a new home, or to a pet shop, before seven weeks of age will not realize its full potential as a dog and companion.

Socialization Period (7-12 Weeks)

The best time to bring a puppy into its new home is during the Socialization Period. At this time he should be introduced to as many things as possible that will play a role in his future life. For example, if you want him to interact peacefully with farm animals or with a cat, it is at this age that he should meet them in a positive, non-threatening manner. If the breeder has not already introduced him to sounds like the vacuum cleaner, engine noises, and city traffic, it is during this period that you should do so. Children, men with beards, women in floppy hats, and senior citizens, while all people to us, appear different to the dog, and he should meet as many different ages and types of people as possible.

At seven weeks of age the puppy's brain has the brain waves of an adult dog. His capacity for concentration, however, is not yet adult, and thus his attention span is quite short. But he can learn. Not only can a young puppy learn, but he will learn, whether he is taught or not. It is at this age that the most rapid learning occurs. Everything he comes in contact with is making a lasting impression on him as it never will again.

Things learned at this age are learned permanently. This is important to think about when you want to hold your tiny puppy on your lap while you watch TV. Remember that he is going to grow up. Do you want him to sit on your lap when he weighs 70 pounds or more?

16

Introduce your puppy to many ages and types of people.

Puppies are ready to learn at 7 weeks.

BOOGA
BOOGA

Remember not to frighten your puppy unnecessarily during the fear period . . .

17

This is the best age to begin your pup's training in a positive, non-punitive manner, taking into account his physical limitations and short attention span. The lessons in the following chapters have been proven effective and successful with puppies as young as seven weeks.

Fear Imprint Period (8-11 Weeks)

During this period any traumatic, painful or frightening experiences will have a more lasting impact on your pup than if they occur at any other time. For instance, a trip to the veterinarian during this period, if unpleasant, could forever make your dog apprehensive about going to the doctor. To avoid this, take along a toy to play with and some treats for your puppy while you wait. Have your veterinarian give treats to the puppy along with loads of petting and praise after completing the examination and inoculations. Under no circumstances should elective surgery such as ear cropping or hernia repair be performed during this period.

In general, avoid stressful situations, but do continue to socialize and train your pup in a nontraumatic way.

Seniority Classification Period (12-16 Weeks)

This critical period is also known as the "Age of Cutting"—cutting teeth and cutting the apron strings.

It is at this age that your pup will begin testing to see who the pack leader is going to be. From 12 weeks on, if your puppy makes an attempt to bite you, even in seeming play, or bites the leash while you are walking or training, it is usually an attempt to dominate. Biting behavior should be completely and absolutely discouraged from 13 weeks on. (See "Biting" in Chapter 12, Behavior Problems.)

Serious training, if not already started, should begin now. It will establish, in a manner easy for the pup to understand, that you are the leader. When you assume responsibility for having a dog, you assume responsibility for training and for being the pack leader. Pack leadership is something you will learn through training—through specific exercises designed to teach your dog that you are in charge.

The critical periods above are generally the same, regardless of the breed or size of your dog. The ages of the next critical periods may vary depending upon the size of the dog. In general, smaller dogs tend to experience these periods earlier than large dogs.

Flight Instinct Period (4-8 Months)

This is the age when your puppy will truly test his wings: He will venture off on his own and turn a completely deaf ear when you call. If this occurs during training, the pup's response to your "Come" command will be

18

to take off in the opposite direction. Now you know why, and you can say to yourself, "Aha! Flight Instinct!"

The Flight Instinct Period generally lasts for anywhere from several weeks to a month, and how you handle your dog at this time will mean the difference between a dog who ignores your call and one who responds readily. Following the lessons in this book will enable you to deal with this situation, but for now, remember, until you are pretty sure your dog has been trained, keep him on leash. Putting him in a position where he can run away from you will only serve to ingrain this undesirable behavior.

Second Fear Imprint Period (6-14 Months)

This Fear Imprint Period is not as well defined as the first one which occurs between eight and eleven weeks. It is marked by your now adolescent dog's reluctance to approach something new or his sudden fear of something familiar. To get through this period, be patient, be kind, don't force your pup to do something frightening to him and, above all, continue your training so that he is being given leadership in a familiar and reassuring manner.

Maturity (1-4 Years)

This critical period is often marked by an increase in aggression and by a renewed testing of your leadership. The increased aggression is not necessarily negative. Often it means that a previously over-friendly dog becomes a good watch dog and barks when people come to the door. It may also mean, however, that Konrad and Argus, who used to be good friends, are now fighting every time they see each other.

If, at maturity, your dog tries again to test your leadership, handle him firmly and continue training. Train your dog regularly throughout this testing period, praising for the proper response. If he develops a real problem, consult the chapter on Behavior Problems. If you feel he is too much for you, you may have to seek professional help.

Many dogs will not undergo any noticeable changes during these time periods. But, just as children go through the "terrible twos" with textbook predictability, you should be prepared for the psychological changes that will occur in your dog, so that you understand what is happening and can help him, and yourself, get through this time.

FICTION AND FACT ABOUT HOW THE DOG LEARNS

How Konrad Does *Not* Learn

Dogs are such popular pets because they have so many seemingly human qualities. They are honest—dogs don't lie; they're trustworthy—at

The greatest mistake that can be committed, is to endow the dog with a set of human morals and values and expect him to live up to them.

Konrad understands only that you are upset with him, but he does not understand it's because of the steak he ate.

least once they have been trained; and they are loyal (who can forget Buck in Jack London's *Call of the Wild*?) Dogs are social creatures who enjoy our company as much as we enjoy theirs. In times of need they comfort us, and in general mirror our moods.

Precisely because dogs have so many of these qualities, care must be taken not to attribute human traits to the dog which he does not possess. The dog is *a*moral. This simply means he does not know right from wrong. Even when trained, he does not understand why he may not lie on the couch. Perhaps the single greatest injustice that can be committed against the dog is to endow him with a set of human moral values, to expect him to live up to these values, and to punish him for failure to do so.

A thorough understanding of what can be expected from a dog is helpful, but understanding what we cannot expect is critical. A dog will not, for example, do something or refrain from doing something out of a sense of duty, gratitude or conscience. As much as we would like to think otherwise, a dog is an animal—by no means dumb, but an animal nevertheless.

What about the dog, you ask, who has done something naughty and has guilt written all over him? Why is he acting guilty if he does not know he did something wrong? It is because of his owner's attitude. It is not guilt that he is feeling, but apprehension and fear. The scenario goes something like this: Konrad has mutilated one of your favorite slippers. After you discover the evil deed, you summon Konrad at once. On the basis of prior experiences Konrad knows that tone of voice only too well—it is always followed by a thrashing. Hesitatingly Konrad appears, expecting the worst. Sure enough, after being confronted with the evidence, he is thrashed once again.

So it is not guilt you saw, but apprehension, pure and simple. If you don't believe us, try this little experiment: drop a Kleenex on the floor, call your dog and point to it. Use the same tone of voice containing that barely suppressed rage and "wait till I get my hands on you" tone you have used in the past for such occasions. Even though your dog has done nothing wrong, he will look guilty.

Attempting to shame a dog for what you consider a transgression on his part will not get the message across either. Of course he reacts to whatever words are spoken and gives the appearance of being thoroughly remorseful. But does he understand what it's all about?

Consider this example: You are preparing supper. A succulent steak is on the counter and you go to the pantry for some other ingredients. Konrad, who up to now has been sleeping in the corner, knows that opportunity knocks only once. He snatches the steak and quickly devours it. When you return you immediately see what has happened. Konrad is summoned, "Shame on you! How could you?" Konrad looks dutifully ashamed of himself. Does he understand why? The answer is no. Konrad understands only that you are upset with him, but he does not understand that it is because of the steak he ate. Again, his doleful appearance is created by your attitude toward him and not by remorse for his misdeed. No doubt he thoroughly enjoyed the steak.

Efforts to reason with your dog will also be singularly unsuccessful. While dogs can think and work out certain things for themselves, they are unable to reason as we can. Even though many dog owners are convinced that "he understands every word I say," the dog is unable to respond either to promises of future reward for good behavior or threats of impending punishment for bad behavior. Admonishments such as, "If you do that one more time I'll wring your neck!" are as futile as the promise "If you behave yourself while I'm gone, I'll give you a hamburger."

How *Does* Konrad Learn?

Now that we know what we cannot expect, we may address ourselves to how the dog does learn. The dog learns through experience. The number of times a particular action must be repeated for a dog to learn and to commit it to memory varies. If the dog perceives the action as being particularly advantageous to him, he may learn it on the basis of one experience.

Picture a household which has just acquired a three-year-old dog named Cresty. This household has a cat which has learned to help herself to between-meal snacks by opening and entering the cabinet where the cat food is kept. Cresty watches in utter astonishment as the cat goes through her routine. After the cat has left, Cresty also tries to open the cabinet. After several tries she is successful and helps herself to a mouthful of cat food. Because she viewed it as highly advantageous to herself—the reward being a few kibbles of cat food—it took Cresty only one experience to learn this little maneuver.

Similarly, the dog learns to avoid particularly disadvantageous situations on the basis of one experience. Like the child who touches the hot stove, the dog will shy from activities that have previously produced discomfort or fear.

The actions or exercises we teach our dogs in training are not, in themselves, viewed by the dog as either advantageous or disadvantageous. For training to succeed, we must clearly distinguish in terms understandable to the dog what is to his advantage and what is not. Once the dog perceives that it is to his benefit both to refrain from conduct we consider objectionable and to adopt those actions we consider desirable, he learns very quickly.

Witness the following: Konrad likes to chase the cat, and his intentions are not honorable. When the cat enters the room, Konrad's attention is immediately focused on her. We know from past experience that whenever Konrad gets that look in his eyes, he is thinking about giving chase. It is at

22

The trained dog has advantages and freedom denied to the untrained dog . . .

that very instant that we impress upon him that the abandonment of such ideas is to his advantage.

Primary Inducements

The objective of obedience training is the ability to communicate your desires to your dog in a manner that does not violate his dignity and which results in a harmonious and mutually enjoyable relationship. In practical terms this means on- and off-leash control, the benefits of which are considerable. Think about the freedom a trained dog has: he can be allowed to run off leash, retrieve a ball or stick; accompany his master for nice walks and in every sense becomes a member of the family. Most of this freedom is denied to the untrained dog because he won't come when called, he won't bring the ball back, and nobody takes him for walks because he pulls so much. He is usually confined or left on a line and is ignored.

Training is accomplished by creating an association between primary inducements and secondary inducements. Primary inducements are those directly responsible for a given response by the dog—either voluntary or involuntary. For example, you can coax most dogs to come to you by kneeling down. Your reduced body posture elicits a voluntary response by the dog to come to you. If, on the other hand, you have your dog on a 15-foot line and you want him to come to you, all you have to do is reel him in. The response in that case would be involuntary.

Voluntary responses are elicited through encouragement, body posture and food, all of which are perceived by the dog as pleasant, with food obviously being the most gratifying. He will learn, through repetition, that a food reward, a word of praise or a pat on the head are positive experiences associated with having pleased us. Through such repetitions this becomes a conditioned response and can aid us in our training. The approach to training described in this book relies primarily on voluntary responses, particularly during the initial learning stages and is called inducive training. However, because it is neither feasible nor reliable to train a dog by purely inducive methods, some of our training, called compulsive training, relies on involuntary responses.

Compulsion is here defined as the state of being forced to perform some action which appears to be without reason. Compulsion ranges from mild, which is not unpleasant, to strong, which can be highly unpleasant. Physically placing the dog into a sit is an example of mild compulsion. Checking the dog on leash—a quick jerk on the training collar and an immediate release—is an example of strong compulsion.

Compulsion can be used to train a dog both to do something and to refrain from doing something. For example, it can be used to teach a dog to heel, which is walking at the handler's left side, or to stay, which is not to move.

24

When compulsion is used to train the dog to perform an exercise it is immediately followed by a pleasant experience such as praise or a treat. By alternating between pleasant experiences—praise or food—and unpleasant experiences—compulsion—the dog learns that the adoption of a particular course of action is to his advantage. In the initial stages of teaching any exercise, strong compulsion should be avoided so as not to intimidate the dog.

When compulsion is used to teach the dog to refrain from some activity, it is not followed by praise. Otherwise we would be praising the dog, albeit inadvertently, at the precise moment that he is thinking about continuing the undesired activity. Remember Konrad and the cat. After having impressed upon him to leave the cat alone, this would not be followed by praise because as long as the cat is in sight, Konrad may still be thinking about doing some bodily harm to the poor kitty. Praise would only encourage him to follow through on his evil designs.

When training the dog to refrain from some activity, the degree of compulsion used should be such that it does not have to be repeated more than once or twice. Guidance along these lines will be provided in the section on discipline.

Secondary Inducements

Secondary inducements are commands or signals. During the training process, the dog is conditioned by repetition to associate the secondary inducement with the primary inducement. For example, you can induce your dog to assume the sitting position by means of a treat, at the same time saying "Sit." By repeating the procedure, the dog commits to memory what is expected of him, and learns to respond to the secondary inducement—the word "Sit." The dog is considered trained once he responds reliably to the secondary inducement, the command.

A word of caution: Continued reliance on secondary inducements alone, even when the dog has learned them, will ultimately render the dog unreliable because the association between the primary inducement and the secondary inducement begins to weaken. For example, once the dog has been trained to respond to the command "Sit," he does fine for a while. But then he begins to sit less quickly than he used to. He requires a second command, and soon a third, until he gets to the point where he acts as if he's never heard the word "Sit." What has happened is that the association between the primary and the secondary inducement has become weaker with successive repetitions of the command without the primary inducement. To prevent the weakening of the association, it will have to be reestablished from time to time.

How quickly the association weakens depends on the dog and the exercise. Some exercises must be reinforced frequently by means of the

The more instinctive the task, the quicker it will be learned . . .

primary inducement and others only sparingly. To keep the dog reliable, however, all exercises require periodic reinforcement.

INFLUENCES ON LEARNING

Breed Characteristics

One question we are often asked is how long should it take for a dog to learn a particular exercise. The answer is that it depends on the dog and the exercise. The ease or difficulty with which a given exercise will be learned by your dog will vary with the extent to which the exercise is in harmony with his instincts. The more instinctive the required task, the quicker it will be learned. Conversely, the less instinctive the action desired, the longer it will take to learn.

You will understand more about the way your dog responds to training by familiarizing yourself with the functions for which his breed was developed. In the case of a mixed-breed, the dog's response to training will resemble one of his pure-bred progenitors. For example, a herding dog, such as a Shetland Sheepdog, can be taught to heel more quickly than a hunting dog like a Beagle. A sporting dog like a Golden Retriever can be taught to retrieve more quickly than one of the Northern breeds, such as a Siberian Husky. Most dogs can be taught to stay more quickly than a Terrier.

Should you run into difficulties in your training, examine what you are trying to teach your dog in light of his breed characteristics. What your neighbor's dog learns in a few sessions may take your dog several weeks.

Your Attitude

By far the most important influence on learning is your attitude toward the dog. A positive and benevolent attitude on your part sets the stage for maximum cooperation on his part. Dogs have a keen perception of their environment and are strongly affected by it. In quiet and pleasant surroundings the dog will respond in a relaxed and willing manner. An atmosphere the dog perceives as unsettling or threatening will cause anxiety and apprehension, both impediments to learning. A discordant home, a move, a death in the family, or any crisis will be unsettling to your dog.

There will be times in your training when you feel disappointed, frustrated, and even angry. When this happens, your dog will become anxious and apprehensive because dogs have difficulty coping with such human emotions. When you feel this way, stop, compose yourself and resume training when you have regained the proper outlook.

To become successful in your training, banish the notion that your dog is wrong. If he fails to respond to a command, or if he does something you

Cute now . . .

. . . but what about then?

don't want him to do, it is your responsibility to train him to respond or to refrain from the undesired action. The dog's behavior is largely the end result of his upbringing—he misbehaves only because you permit him to. To a great extent your dog's behavior—good, bad or indifferent—is the product of your efforts. By following the motto "the dog is never wrong" you will avoid becoming emotional about your dog's responses. If he makes a mistake it is not because he is spiteful but because he needs more training.

Naturally there are limitations as to what you can expect from your dog, and the rule of reason must apply. Your dog may be perfectly house-trained, but that does not mean he can hold on forever. Leaving your dog longer than eight hours without a chance to relieve himself is unreasonable, and any accident which occurs would be your fault. The golden rule to follow is: *Avoid putting the dog in a position where he can make a mistake.* Once you accept the fact that errors are your fault, his education can proceed on a sound basis.

Consistency

Dogs don't understand gray areas such as "sometimes," "not very often," "hardly ever," "perhaps," or "maybe." If you normally permit your dog on the couch, you can't expect him to stay off when you have guests or just because his paws are muddy. This is an example of a gray area, or inconsistency beyond his comprehension. Dogs understand black and white, yes and no, pleasant and unpleasant, and that the couch is off limits—period.

An accountant named David consulted us about Sahib, his Afghan. One rainy day, Sahib jumped on David, not only muddying his three-piece suit, but also knocking his attache case to the ground. The case opened, and all his books and papers fell in the mud. Needless to say, David wanted to put a stop to this kind of behavior.

Upon further questioning we discovered that David usually changed his clothes before greeting Sahib. Once in his jeans, he didn't mind Sahib's jumping and, in fact, even encouraged it. David did not realize that Sahib could not tell the difference between play clothes and working clothes. To Sahib, jumping was jumping—distinctions between jeans and dress clothes meant nothing to him.

For David the choice was clear: If he didn't want to risk being jumped on by Sahib when in good clothes, he would have to be consistent and train the dog not to jump at all.

Body Sensitivity

Your dog's seeming willingness to learn is also influenced by his body sensitivity: that is, how readily he responds to the training collar. Dogs range from highly sensitive to very insensitive. Age and size do not usually affect body sensitivity, although in some instances the mature dog will be somewhat more insensitive than the puppy.

Body sensitivity is affected by the dog's activity or interest at a given moment. A Beagle on the trail of a rabbit will not feel brambles, just as a fighting dog appears to be oblivious to pain.

Breed characteristics and the strength of a dog's instincts will also influence body sensitivity. Keeping a Beagle's nose off the ground while teaching it to heel requires herculean efforts seemingly out of all proportion to the size of the dog.

This particular aspect of training will be covered in more detail in the section dealing with selection of training equipment. Here it will suffice to say that your dog's response to your efforts to train him, or lack thereof, will dictate the type of training collar you will have to use in order to be successful.

When Do I Start?

One question many people have is, "What is the best age at which to start training a dog?" The answer is at seven weeks of age. At this age the puppy's brain waves are the same as the adult dog's, but without the experience. It is also during its early development that the puppy is most eager to learn and learns quickly, with a minimum of effort on your part.

Training a young dog, and especially a puppy, is preferable to waiting until the dog is older for two important reasons. First, the puppy is much more easily managed physically than a full-grown dog and so is well within the capability of the budding trainer. Second, the puppy will learn while growing up, either on his own or what we teach him.

In the first case, it is the very ability to physically manage and control the puppy or young dog which makes it so very easy to procrastinate and put off his education. But the day of reckoning comes all too soon—all of a sudden he is full-grown and wants to do everything his way. It is far simpler to train him before he gets to this stage.

In the second instance, the puppy left to his own devices will develop habits we do not want him to learn. Again, it is much easier to train the puppy to behave correctly before he has learned any bad habits than to have to retrain him later. Retraining takes much longer than it does to train him properly in the first place.

Of course, puppies do not have the same motor coordination as the mature dog, and allowances will have to be made in that regard. But

30

clumsiness is not the same as an inability to learn. So make it easy for yourself—begin training your puppy as soon as possible.

While training is easier if begun early, a dog can be trained no matter what his age. The saying, "You can't teach an old dog new tricks," is an old wives' tale. It may take longer and require more effort to train an older dog, but the end result will justify your efforts.

Unintentional Training

Another influence on learning is unintentional training, which takes place when we think we are teaching the dog one thing, when in reality we are teaching him something different.

Bill called us one day, upset by the fact that Rasso, his 12-week-old Rottweiler, would not come when he called him. Not only would Rasso not come, but he would take off for parts unknown as soon as Bill said the word "come."

Upon further questioning, we discovered the following: Whenever Rasso had an accident in the house he was angrily summoned by Bill, confronted with the mess, and soundly thrashed. After having repeated this procedure several times, Bill began to notice that when he called, Rasso ran away and hid under the couch. By thrashing Rasso for having an accident in the house, Bill thought he was housetraining him. Actually, he was training him to run away and hide when called.

Taking this one step further, you should not call a dog to you and follow his arrival with anything he perceives as unpleasant. For example, don't call your dog to you to cut his nails, give him a heartworm pill, or lock him up, without some intervening *pleasant* experience like a treat and praise.

Roughhousing with your puppy can also lead to unintentional training because it teaches the puppy to assert itself against you, not a desirable result at all.

A more subtle form of unintentional training occurs when we pet the puppy or dog to calm it down from signs of fear or aggression. In either case, petting or stroking the dog while using what is intended to be soothing language such as, "That's all right," "You're okay, good dog," will only serve to reinforce and foster the behavior.

Gwen liked to take her Doberman, Elsa, for a walk, but Elsa would growl and snap at other dogs they met on the street. When asked to describe what she did under those circumstances, she told us that she would stroke Elsa, telling her that the strange dog meant her no harm, and that she was okay and in no danger.

Roughhousing with your puppy

. . . may lead to undesirable results later on.

In trying to soothe Elsa, Gwen was unintentionally encouraging the aggressive behavior through her praising, soothing words and petting.

The other extreme would be Konrad hiding behind his owner when a stranger approaches, whereupon he would be petted reassuringly and told that the stranger means no harm. Konrad in turn interprets the praise and petting as a reward for having done the right thing—that is, to be afraid and hide behind his owner.

There are many other examples of unintentional training and some of them will be covered in the actual lessons. For now, you only have to remember this: Dogs learn by repetition. Every time you permit an incorrect response, the dog is learning that response. So make sure you don't unintentionally permit or encourage incorrect responses.

Where Does Konrad Live?

Your dog's living arrangements also influence his learning. The best guidance we can give you is to avoid both extremes—extended isolation or constant togetherness. If your dog has to be alone for prolonged periods, he will be too excited when you return to pay much attention to his lesson. Give him a chance to be with you for a while and to calm down before you start training.

If your dog is with you almost constantly, training will not have much appeal for him. A few hours rest from human companionship—by himself in the yard or a room—will heighten his desire to be with you and make him a more eager student.

Other extremes such as keeping a dog chained or carrying it around all the time, also adversely affect your dog's outlook on training. It will be difficult to convince the dog who is carried everywhere that heeling is fun.

Physical Condition

It is easy to see when a dog is in *obvious* discomfort and not up to training. But many conditions which cause discomfort are *not* clearly visible and also impede the dog's ability and willingness to learn. Examples are ear infections, long toenails, and mats. We will discuss these under "Grooming" in Chapter 4.

Some other examples of physical conditions which will affect your dog's willingness to learn are tonsilitis, hip dysplasia, and infected or impacted anal glands. If your dog is refusing to do something he previously did willingly, it may be that he is uncomfortable due to an unseen ailment which requires veterinary attention.

Doris had been training her Cocker Spaniel, Quincy, for several weeks when she first began having a problem during the heeling exercise. Quincy would climb the leash, rise up on his hind legs, and place both forelegs over the leash. It turned out that Quincy had tonsilitis, and the pressure of the collar against his throat was quite painful. Climbing the leash was Quincy's way of relieving the pressure on his neck and telling Doris that something was wrong.

In this case, once the physical condition cleared up, training resumed without further difficulty.

Occasionally behavior resulting from a physical ailment becomes a learned response which will continue even after the original problem has been cured. For example, Alex also had tonsilitis and manifested the same behavior as Quincy, except that in Alex's case it went undiagnosed for almost a month, during which time the owner continued to attempt to train Alex. Even after the tonsilitis had been cured, Alex would continue the same leash-climbing activity because it had become a learned response. It took several weeks of consistent training before the behavior stopped.

If your dog has a structural fault, hip dysplasia for instance, the act of sitting may be uncomfortable for him. He may need to adjust his weight as he sits, thereby taking longer to position himself than would a dog without this condition. Your veterinarian can x-ray your dog to evaluate his hips if you suspect there is something structurally wrong.

Infected or impacted anal glands will affect not only your dog's willingness to sit, but his entire outlook on life. Your veterinarian can show you how to deal with this common problem.

Hormonal development of the growing dog will cause periods of what we call "flaky" behavior while going into adolescence and again while going into maturity. It is best to be patient and understanding during these times.

Unspayed bitches are prone to additional flaky behavior. Prior to, during, and approximately two months after their heat, they are subject to extreme mood fluctuations. Again, be patient and understanding, and your female will become her old self again.

These are just some examples to alert you to some physical causes of behavioral changes. Whenever you notice a change in your dog's behavior, suspect a physical reason first.

Discipline

One of the most baffling questions to the new, and even some not-so-new, dog owners seems to be, "What is the right way to discipline my dog?" It would be presumptuous to say there is only one right way, for so much depends on the specific circumstances.

We have always felt that the mother dog knows best. She does not nag; she does not threaten; she does not plead. Discipline is swift and physical, firm but loving, and always just the right amount to get the job done. It ranges from a snarling snap to a shake by the scruff of the neck. The puppy is never confused and knows exactly what Mother expects.

Before providing some specific guidelines for the dog owner, we should first clarify the circumstances under which discipline in the proper sense is used. At the beginning of this chapter we explained that dog training is a term used to describe two distinct activities. The first is to teach a dog to do something he would not do on his own, and the second is to inhibit him from activities he would do on his own, but which we consider objectionable.

It is in the second instance that discipline is used. Discipline is *not* used in training the dog to do something he would not do on his own.

Discipline is used in the following manner:

1) For many dogs, a barklike and emphatic verbal reprimand such as "Stop it!" will suffice in most circumstances, especially if this is started when the dog is a puppy. For example, as a puppy, Konrad developed a keen and not uncommon interest in the garbage. Every time he attempted to investigate, he heard a stern "Stop it!" After several repetitions, Konrad learned to leave the garbage alone.

To be effective, this reprimand must be uttered once, sharply, and at the onset of the offending behavior. It would be ineffective in this instance to wait until Konrad had already eaten some tasty garbage, and then to try convincing him that it was bad by either yelling at and/or hitting him.

2) Young puppies respond very well to a firm shake by the scruff, the loose skin at the back, of the neck. This is how the mother dog disciplines her pups. At the same time, a verbal "Stop it!" imitates the growl that Mom would utter. Again, this must be done as the immediate consequence of an undesirable action. For instance, Konrad is playing with you and the play gets a little out of hand. He starts biting at your hands and arms, and you wish him to stop. A shake by the scruff with "Stop it!" is an effective disciplinary measure for this situation.

We should mention here that under those circumstances shaking your finger at the puppy while saying, "nonononowhatanaughtypuppyhowmanytimesdoihavetotellyoublahblah," is not only useless as a disciplinary measure, but will have the opposite effect. That is, it will encourage the puppy to snap at your finger.

3) Another approach to discipline, especially effective with prepubescent dogs and young adults, is to grasp the hair and loose skin at the side of the neck near the face with both hands, one on each side, lift the dog's front end off the ground, establish eye contact, and say "Stop it!" Maintain eye contact until the dog looks away, and then release your hold.

While being brushed one day, Konrad decided he had had enough. He tried to bite the brush, wiggled and squirmed and would not stay in one place. After having been told in no uncertain terms, as above, that this was unacceptable behavior, the grooming session proceeded without incident.

4) The most severe form of discipline we use is a smart smack on the *top* of the muzzle, administered with either the hand or the loop end of the leash. It is reserved for checking instances of aggression, either toward people or other animals. Remember Konrad and the cat? It was this form of discipline that was used to convince him not to chase the cat.

Whichever disciplinary measure the situation calls for, if three tries on your part do not produce the desired response, you are either not doing it correctly, or you are using the wrong technique under the particular circumstance. Discipline must be swift and cannot leave the slightest doubt in the dog's mind that you will not accept this behavior. Under *no* circumstances should you repeatedly pummel the dog in a fit of rage.

In addition to the mechanics of discipline, timing is important. The ideal time to discipline a dog is when he is thinking about the offensive conduct. **The further removed in point of time, the less effective the discipline will be.**

Recall, once again, the example of Konrad and the cat. Konrad was disciplined for *thinking* about giving chase, long before he had the opportunity to follow through. Had Konrad succeeded in chasing the cat, discipline after the fact would be useless and would undermine your relationship with your dog. Once Konrad has enjoyed the chase, there is nothing you can do to make him *un*enjoy it.

Remember when Konrad stole the steak and was later chastised? Suppose Konrad has another opportunity to steal a steak a few days later. Will he? You bet he will. In his mind there is absolutely no association between the act of stealing and eating the steak and your subsequent displeasure with him. To be effective, discipline in this instance must come before Konrad even takes the steak, preferably when he is thinking about taking the steak.

When you consider discipline, keep in mind how the dog learns and, above all, be just.

Location

Another influence on how the dog learns is location. The dog may associate a particularly unpleasant experience with the place where it happened.

Iris was walking Moe on leash from the car to the house, when she accidentally tripped over the leash, startling Moe. For the next few weeks Moe would jump over the spot where Iris had tripped because he associated the location with being startled, and not with Iris' clumsiness.

While the dog is still behaving apprehensively about this location, it would be a poor choice for a training site.

Sequence of Exercises

The exercises that you will teach your dog basically consist of two types. The first are action exercises such as heeling, retrieving, and coming when called. The second are control exercises such as lying down and standing still.

Control exercises are not as much fun for the dog as action exercises are and in many instances may have a depressing effect on him. As a general rule, you should not practice two control exercises such as the DOWN and the STAND in succession.

On the other hand, if you have an extremely bouncy dog, you should not practice two action exercises in succession. What you are looking for is just the right mix of enthusiasm and control.

Each lesson is followed by a lesson checklist which has been put into a specific order to take this mix into account. Depending on your individual circumstances, you may have to modify this order of exercises.

CONCLUSION

This chapter has outlined what you can and what you cannot expect from your dog, how your dog learns, and the various influences on learning. You would be well advised, as you proceed in your training, to periodically review this chapter to refresh your recollection, particularly when things don't seem to be going as well as you think they should. The understanding you now possess about your dog gives you a good foundation to be successful in your efforts to train him.

Dog training is a rewarding and satisfying undertaking that is fun for both you and your dog. The following eight lessons represent a total of eight weeks training—a small price to pay for the many years of enjoyment you will have with a trained dog.

2

You and Your Dog

MANY DOG OWNERS have acquired dogs with the aid of puppy aptitude testing which has gained popularity in recent years. On the basis of a Puppy Personality Profile, a highly accurate assessment can be made of the adult dog's temperament. The main purpose of the Puppy Personality Profile is to minimize the risk of disappointment resulting from an incompatible match. Through testing, done at 7 weeks of age, the right puppy can be placed in the right home, and the owner's needs and expectations can be met. See Bibliography.

Regardless of how you have acquired your puppy or dog, we hope that with the aid of this book you will enjoy a mutually rewarding relationship with your dog for many years.

In this chapter we will briefly highlight some important aspects of having a dog that are not covered in the lessons.

What Does Konrad Eat?

With the literally thousands of dog foods on the market, and the barrage of television commercials, it is difficult for the dog owner to make a rational, informed decision about what is best to feed a dog. While we have personally chosen to make our own dog food rather than feed a commercially available brand, we understand that not everyone is prepared to do this. For those of you who are interested in this food, or who would like to be able to make an informed choice in the selection of a commercial dog food, see the Bibliography.

We will limit our discussion of dog food to three broad categories: canned, semi-moist, and dry. All three can, and often will, contain artificial

38

What does Konrad eat?

color and other additives to which many dogs are allergic, often causing behavior problems.

Canned dog food is about 75% water. Therefore, if your dog needs to eat 1 pound of food each day, and you feed him a 1-pound can of dog food, he is really eating only about 25%, or a quarter, of a pound of food.

The semi-moist varieties, while being very convenient, contain large amounts of preservatives, salt, and sugar. Sugar is a major cause of obesity and hyperactivity. Salt increases the need for water, and feeding this type of food may make your housetraining efforts more difficult.

If you are going to feed a commercial dog food, you should only select one that is labeled "Complete and Balanced." If it is a dry food, it should also have a meat protein source as one of its first three ingredients.

A dog is affected by nutrition just as we are, and we have traced many behavior and training problems to nutritional deficiencies of one kind or another. Lethargy, hyperactivity, aggression and shyness are frequently the result of improper diet. If your dog is suffering from such a dietary deficiency, it will drastically limit your choices of commercial dog foods. You may wind up making your own, as we do.

Changing your dog's diet may upset his system, causing diarrhea. It should therefore be done over a period of a week or so by mixing gradually increasing amounts of the new food with the old.

Once you have selected a dog food, stick with it. Dogs do not need variety. If he stops eating for a day or two, don't worry—it's not going to do the healthy dog any harm. Too much concern about eating is just as bad as not enough, so don't become obsessed about how your dog eats. We feed twice a day, and if it's not gone within 10 minutes, Konrad is not hungry. If he does not eat for several days, consult your veterinarian.

Housetraining

Housetraining is a tremendously important part of every house dog's life. It is also an area which abounds with misinformation and old wive's tales. Because housetraining is one of the first lessons you will be teaching your puppy, it sets the stage for future training. To avoid undermining your relationship before you have really had a chance to establish it, it is important that housetraining be nonpunitive and nontraumatic.

Before you begin housetraining your dog, keep the following in mind: prior to the age of 3 to 4 months, a puppy does not have the ability to control himself for very long. His sphincter and bladder control are minimal. As he matures, he will gain more control of his bodily functions, but an 8 or 10-week-old puppy cannot go very long between bathroom trips. Many people believe that, because their puppy can last through the night, he should be able to make it through the entire day. This is not true. The body's functions slow down at night; so all of us, your puppy included, do not need to go to the bathroom.

In general, puppies will have to go to the bathroom upon waking (even from a short nap), after eating, after drinking, during or after play and excitement, during or after chewing, when they are sniffing in a circling fashion (they are probably looking for a good place to go), and at other times, just because it's been a while since they've gone.

The following positive approach to housetraining will greatly facilitate this aspect of your pup's training, and will minimize the need to clean up. We call these the Ten Commandments of Housetraining:

1)   Feed at set times. Do not vary your schedule, even on weekends. If you feed at 7:00 a.m. on a weekday, feed at that same time on Saturday and Sunday, at least until he is housetrained.

2)   Feed one diet and do not vary it. Do not feed table scraps or treats during the housetraining period.

3)   Watch your puppy's stools to make sure they are well formed. If they are loose, you may be overfeeding.

4)   Have your veterinarian do a stool check for worms, and if your puppy has worms, follow your veterinarian's advice to rid him of them.

5)   Take your puppy out on a regular schedule, stay out with him, and praise him when he goes.

6)   When you take him out, go straight to one spot and stand there. Do not walk with him. Teach him that this is the time and place for him to go to the bathroom.

7)   When your puppy has an accident in the house, clean it with a cleaner designed for urine odor, or with white vinegar and water. Do not use an ammonia-based cleaner. Urine contains ammonia and such a cleaner would attract your dog to that spot again.

8)   If you catch your puppy in the act of going to the bathroom in the house, say "STOP!" Pick him up, carry him directly outside to his toilet area, and wait with him until he goes there. Praise.

9)   Keep a chart of exactly what your puppy does at what time, including accidents. You will notice a pattern and be better able to plan his schedule.

10)   If you don't catch him in the act, but come upon an accident after he has finished, even if he has just finished, say nothing. Put your puppy in another area so you can clean it up. It will not do any good, and it will do harm, to tell your puppy how angry you are that he went to the bathroom. He will not understand why you are angry; it will only confuse him and cause him to fear you. Dogs cannot make an association between the puddle on the floor and the physical need to go to the bathroom.

Under no circumstances ever should you drag your puppy over to an accident to show it to him and scold him or, worst of all, rub his nose in it. This will not facilitate housetraining. It will undermine your relationship

Housetraining your puppy.

with your dog, and it is unsanitary and disgusting. Dogs punished in this manner may get housetrained, but it is in spite of the punishment, not because of it. Dogs are generally quite clean and will try to go to the bathroom outside, once they are physically able to and once they understand what you desire. It doesn't have to be unpleasant for either one of you.

Using this approach to housetraining, your attitude should be one of patience and positive thinking. If anything goes wrong, treat it as your fault—you didn't keep a close enough eye on him; you weren't quick enough to get him outside after he woke up; you didn't recognize the signs that he was looking for a spot to go. He is just doing what comes naturally.

When you cannot be with your puppy to supervise him, keep him confined. We recommend that confinement be in a crate, a small cage where your puppy has room to stand up, lie down and turn around. The crate is his bed, and dogs are reluctant to soil their sleeping quarters. If he does have an accident in the crate, do not yell at him or say anything. He has already suffered enough—first trying to hold it and then staying in the crate with his mess.

When he is out of his crate, keep your puppy in an area of the house where you can keep an eye on him so you can take him out to his bathroom area at any sign that he might have to go. You can give him the run of other parts of the house when he has just come in from a successful trip outside. The room or rooms you keep him in should have a nonporous surface that is easy to clean when he has an accident. The less trouble it is for you, the less likely you'll be to lose your temper.

The following is a sample schedule you might follow with a young puppy to facilitate housetraining:

Upon waking:	Walk, Feed, Water, Walk
Noon:	Walk, Feed, Water, Walk
4-5:00 p.m.:	Walk, Feed, Water, Walk
7:00 p.m.:	Water, Walk
Bedtime:	Walk

Withhold water for 3 hours or so before you go to bed.

There will be many other times throughout the day that you will be taking a young puppy out.

HOUSETRAINING THE OLDER DOG

If you have an older puppy or dog who is not housetrained, and you have not used the approach outlined above, begin doing so. With the older puppy (5 months or more) or the grown dog, keep him confined in a crate when you are not around to supervise. Everything else remains the same— take him out, praise him for going, ignore accidents, feed on a regular schedule, and obey the Ten Commandments of Housetraining.

If you are having trouble housetraining your dog, in many cases the dog food you are feeding is part of the problem. Some dog foods contain large amounts of filler, nondigestible additives which do nothing for your dog but add to the amount of bulk that must come out. Semi-moist foods, which contain large amounts of salt, cause your dog to drink a great deal of water. This can undermine your housetraining effort. In general, if it looks to you as though your dog is eliminating as much as he is eating, he is not digesting enough of his dog food. Read "What Does Konrad Eat?" and switch him over to a better-quality dog food.

CRATE TRAINING

The advantages of crate training are manifold. It is an invaluable aid in housetraining your dog and in solving behavior problems such as chewing. Traveling in a car with your dog is safer for both you and him if he is crated. It is a lot less risky to leave him in a crate in a hotel room when you go to dinner without having to worry about his destroying the surroundings in his apprehension that you have left him.

There may come a time in your dog's life when he will have to stay at the veterinarian's, where he will be crated. This will be far less traumatic to him if he is used to staying in a crate.

The crate does not represent a prison to your dog. On the contrary, your dog will come to look upon the crate as a refuge, a den, a place to relax and get away from it all. This is especially important if you have children who like to play with your dog—when he has had enough, he must be able to have a place where his privacy will be respected.

Select a crate commensurate with the size of your dog or puppy. It should be large enough for your dog to stand up, turn around, and lie down in comfortably. It should not be so large that your puppy can go to the bathroom at one end and sleep at the other. For example, a crate that would suit a full-grown Mastiff would be an exercise pen for a Mastiff puppy.

Before beginning the training, set the crate up. Take your dog to the crate and let him investigate. Show it to him while talking in a very happy voice. Rattle it a little to show him that it may make noise. You don't want him to first hear the rattle when he is already in the crate and perhaps be frightened because he didn't expect the noise.

Armed with a bowl of treats, begin crate training as follows:

1) Place your dog in the crate with a command such as "get in the crate" or "go to bed" said in a very happy voice. Once in, praise excitedly and give him a treat. Immediately let him out. Repeat three to five times or until your dog is getting into the crate with very little physical guidance.

2) Command your dog into the crate, praise, give him the treat and close the door with him inside. Scratch him through the side of the crate,

If all else fails you can always try placing the dog in the crate from the top.

Crate training.

tell him how wonderful he is, and let him out. Repeat this step five times.

3) Command your dog into the crate, praise, give him the treat, shut the door and leave the room for 5 seconds. Return, tell him how wonderful he is, and let him out. Repeat five times.

4) Command your dog into the crate, praise, give him the treat, shut the door, and leave the room for 10 seconds, then 20, then 1 minute.

5) The final step is to put your dog in the crate, praise, give him the treat and leave the house.

The quickest way to accustom a dog to a crate is to keep it in the bedroom and crate him at night. This also facilitates housetraining.

Remember these important rules for crating a dog:

A)   During the training process, always give the dog a treat for getting in the crate.

B)   Do not be apprehensive or apologetic to your dog for putting him in the crate. Be very matter-of-fact about it. He won't view it as punishment unless he senses that you do.

C)   Never let your dog out of the crate when he is barking. This will be rewarding him for barking, and in a very few repetitions, he will learn that barking means he can get out of the crate. That is exactly how you teach your dog to bark in the crate. If he is barking, make him be quiet before you let him out of the crate. See the Barking section in Behavior Problems, Chapter 12.

D)   If you are using the crate for housetraining and your dog has an accident in the crate, do not chastise him. He has been punished enough by having to stay in the close quarters with his accident. Simply let him out, take him outside, and then clean up the crate.

E)   Do not use the crate as a form of punishment.

F)   When your dog is not confined in the crate, leave the door open so he can have access to it at will.

Even an older dog can be successfully introduced to a crate. Gail had an untrained 1½-year-old Mastiff returned to her because he was a destructive chewer when left alone. And when a Mastiff is a destructive chewer, that's an expensive proposition. One of the first things Gail did was invest in a very large crate, and proceeded to crate train Argus. Although not yet grown, at that time Argus weighed about 175 pounds. When he decided that he would just as soon not get into the crate, there was very little that Gail could do. What she did was get in the crate herself, show Argus the treat, and entice him to join her—which he did. After several repetitions, Argus willingly went in by himself.

Jack had a similar experience with a full-grown Newfoundland, Arin, whom he wanted to crate train. No matter what he did, Arin refused to get in the crate. So Jack took the top off the crate, lifted Arin into it, gave her a treat, opened the door and let her out. As in the previous case, after several successful repetitions, Arin overcame her aversion and was willing to get into the crate through the door.

When You Have to Board Konrad

There comes a time in most of our lives when we must leave our dog behind while we go away. In general, we prefer to leave a dog with a reputable boarding facility rather than to have a neighbor or friend look after Konrad. We have heard too many stories about friendships being destroyed because of something happening to the dog while in the care of a friend. We don't feel it is worth the risk—and a good boarding facility will take as good, and often better, care of your dog as will a friend or neighbor.

The selection of a boarding facility should be made well in advance of any planned vacation. Visit kennels and check into the facilities and services they offer. Walk through the kennel area, checking it for cleanliness (use your nose as a good indicator of how clean a place is) and availability of fresh water and food.

We prefer a kennel that has individual runs for each boarder rather than cages. Is there fecal matter in the runs? Is your visit after cleaning time, so you can reasonably expect the runs to be clean? How often do they clean and disinfect the runs?

If the proprietor will not let you examine the area where the dogs are kept, regardless of the reason, do not board your dog there. There are no insurance regulations that prevent a prospective customer from checking out the facilities.

In general, unless your veterinarian has a separate boarding facility, we do not recommend boarding your dog with him or her. In many cases, your dog will be housed near dogs that may be unhealthy. Anyway, that's like going to the hospital for a vacation.

If you need more information about this subject, contact the American Boarding Kennel Association, 311 N. Union Blvd., Colorado Springs, CO 80909.

Traveling with Konrad

If you are planning to take your dog along with you on a car vacation, there are some things of which you should be aware. Most states require that your dog have current inoculations against distemper and rabies. If you are planning to take him out of the country, make sure you know what the requirements are before leaving for vacation.

Often a change of water will have the same effect on a dog as it does on people. It is a good idea to bottle water at home to take along. Also, a diet change will have an adverse effect, so take along enough dog food, unless you feed a nationally available brand.

There are many motels that will allow dog owners and their pets to

47

More motels would welcome pets if more owners were considerate and their dogs well behaved.

Traveling with Konrad.

stay; however, many other motels have had negative experiences with dog owners allowing their dogs to make a mess and not cleaning up after them. This goes for not only their bathroom habits, but chewing and leaving hair on the blankets and bedspreads. If you allow your dog on the bed, take along your own bedspread for him.

Throughout your travels with your dog, keep in mind that other dog owners want to take their dogs along too. The impression you make will affect how they are received.

Taking Your Dog to School

Enrolling in dog obedience class can be a rewarding experience for both you and your dog, but choosing the wrong class can make the experience unpleasant for both of you. If you are lucky enough to live in an area where you have a selection, shop around. Observe the class prior to taking your own dog. Things to look for are:

Individual Attention

Is the size of the class such that the instructor or assistants are able to give individual attention when needed?

Pleasant Atmosphere

Is there a relaxed friendly atmosphere in the class? Tension and chaos will affect both your ability to learn as well as your dog's.

Training Philosophy

Is the approach to training used in the class consistent with your own feelings about dog training? You will be unhappy in a class where the instructor wants you to do something to your dog that you are unwilling or reluctant to do.

Instructor Expertise and Ability to Teach

Does the instructor seem knowledgeable about dog training? And beyond that, is the instructor able to communicate his or her knowledge effectively? Having the ability to train a dog does not necessarily mean that that person has the ability to teach other people how to train a dog. Dog training expertise and people instructing ability are two different things.

Be a Good Dog Neighbor

Some people think that the world is divided into Dog People and Non-Dog People, and that Non-Dog People hate, if not Dog People, dogs. If this is true, it is because dog owners are not sufficiently considerate of the feelings of Non-Dog People. If you want to be a good dog neighbor, follow these simple rules:

1) Train your dog so you can control him.

2) Don't let your dog run loose and he won't be able to get into garbage cans or chase cars, cats, bicycles or joggers. Many communities also have leash or dog control laws, and if you permit your dog to run loose, he may wind up at the local pound.

3) Don't let your dog soil your neighbor's lawn or yellow his shrubbery. If he does go in your neighbor's yard, pick up after him.

4) If your dog soils anywhere other than your own property, clean up after him. Keep your own property picked up as well, at least for sanitary reasons.

5) Don't permit your dog to jump on people.

6) Don't permit your dog to make a nuisance of himself by excessive barking.

If all dog owners followed these simple rules, there would be no reason for Non-Dog People to dislike either dogs or their owners.

Konrad's Safety

The benefits of owning a well-trained dog are obvious, but have you ever considered the dangers that living in a modern society present to a dog who is allowed to run loose? Dogs who are unsupervised stand the danger of getting hit by a car. Or the driver may swerve to avoid a dog and injure himself or another person.

Dogs running loose will get into garbage and may eat chicken bones or other items that are harmful to them.

Often a seemingly stray dog will be picked up by a dognapper and sold to a research facility for experimentation.

The bottom line is that allowing your dog to run loose and unsupervised is dangerous for him. It is not, as you might believe, a kind way of giving him freedom. True freedom comes only through training.

The leash and control laws that many communities have were written for the protection of the people. But obeying these laws is definitely for the protection of Konrad.

Should You Breed Sadie?

Sooner or later, every owner of a female dog considers the question of whether or not to breed her. Reasons in favor of breeding may be: all our friends want a puppy just like her; we want another dog just like her; the children should witness the miracle of birth; we'd like to make some money.

All of these are the wrong reasons to breed Sadie. When the time comes to place puppies, your friends will suddenly be unable to take one

DIET DINNER

Spaying your female won't make her fat, only overfeeding will make her fat.

Neutering your male dog will not make him a poor watchdog

just now; there is no guarantee that a puppy would be "just like her." (And what will you do with the other seven puppies?) If you want your children to witness the miracle of birth, buy them fish. You don't have to find responsible homes for guppies.

As far as making money goes, few people do, and the potential costs involved in breeding can be staggering. Have you considered that your female might need a Caesarian? What if a puppy is sick, requiring extensive veterinary care? What if Sadie dies in labor? Are you prepared to be a foster mother?

Breeding dogs can be a time consuming, heart wrenching, frustrating and expensive proposition. Certainly some dog owners have positive and even lucrative dog breeding experiences, but then there is the matter of the dog overpopulation problem. In this country, one million unwanted dogs *per month* are destroyed by animal control facilities.

Spaying and Neutering

Every 6 months or so, Sadie will come into season. For a 3-week period she will be extremely attractive to male dogs. Also during this time, her vulva will swell, and she will have a bloody discharge. Unless you want her to become pregnant, extreme care must be taken during this period to keep Sadie away from male dogs. This may not be easy: we have heard of male dogs breaking through screens and windows, not to mention digging under or jumping over fences to get to a female in season. Obviously, leaving her tied out at this time would be inviting a litter.

Even keeping Sadie inside will present problems. Male dogs, who will be attracted from as far away as several miles, will camp on your front stoop, sometimes growling at you when you try to get into your own house; will get into fights on your front lawn; and will urinate against every available vertical surface.

If you are not going to breed Sadie, the easiest way to eliminate this potential problem is for Sadie to undergo an ovariohysterectomy—commonly referred to as spaying. This is also advisable for reasons of overall health. Your veterinarian can answer any questions you may have on this surgical procedure.

Unless you are going to breed Konrad, it is just as advisable to neuter male dogs as female dogs. Males who have been neutered tend to make better pets: they are less likely to roam; to engage in indoor leg lifting; to mount children and furniture or other objects. They are frequently more affectionate; they are less prone to fighting; and they will not be the dogs camping out on someone else's lawn when the female is in season.

Since Konrad is not going to be bred, neutering him will prevent the frequent frustration he will experience every time he catches a whiff of a female in season.

Your training sessions are more likely to be successful if your dog gets regular exercise + fresh air before training sessions.

Exercise and fresh air.

Contrary to popular belief, spaying and neutering will not cause obesity. Overfeeding causes obesity. Spaying and neutering may cause a reduction in your dog's activity level which in turn means that he or she will require less food to maintain optimal weight.

Neutering your male will not make him less territorially protective. He will still bark at intruders. If you hunt your male, neutering will not affect his hunting ability. On the contrary, he will be better able to keep his mind on the game not the gamine. Females who could not be hunted during their season will be able to work through the entire hunting season.

Spaying and neutering are also recommended for specific behavior problems such as overprotectiveness, aggression, dog fighting, mounting, leg lifting inside, and running away. Often an overly active dog will become calmer as a result of spaying or neutering.

Exercise and Fresh Air

The training of your dog will be directly affected by the amount of exercise and fresh air he gets. If your dog does not get enough exercise, his training will be hampered. He will have too much energy, and you will have greater difficulty controlling him. He should be taken for regular walks. In addition to it being good exercise, your dog's mental health will be aided by his having the opportunity to sniff and explore. This will enable him to satisfy his natural instincts for investigating and identifying his environment through his olfactory sense.

Many people do not realize the importance of sunlight and fresh air for their dogs. Mothers who admonish their children to play in the fresh air will keep their dogs confined in the house. Dogs, too, need to be outside for more than a quick bathroom trip. Sunlight contains many important vitamins which the body absorbs through the skin. For Konrad's overall health, he should have at least 15 minutes of sunlight and fresh air every day.

IDIOSYNCRACIES

Rolling

For reasons not entirely clear, dogs have a habit of rolling in foul-smelling substances. This can be fecal material of another species (a particular favorite seems to be cow dung) and dead birds or fish. The delight they derive from this activity is in direct proportion to our disgust.

The only satisfactory solution we have been able to come up with is to bathe Konrad after such an incident. You could prevent the problem, of course, by keeping him on leash all the time, but that would defeat one of the purposes of training. Once in the act, there is nothing you can do other than physically restrain him and head straight for the water hose.

Greeting Behavior

Another behavior which some people find rather unsettling is the manner in which dogs greet each other. When two strange dogs meet, they will first smell their respective genital areas. The purpose of this is to identify the sex of the stranger.

Often dogs will greet a person with whom they are unfamiliar in a similar manner, which can be embarrassing. To prevent your dog from doing this, follow the instructions for a Jumping problem in Chapter 12, Behavior Problems.

3

Getting Ready

WHO SHOULD TRAIN? One person should be responsible for training the dog. This person will be the pack leader from the dog's point of view. In practical terms, this means that some dogs will not respond to children because they won't accept the child as pack leader. In the case of a particularly dominant dog, some women will run into the same problem.

All members of the family are encouraged to read this book so that the dog is handled with consistency. For instance, if Mom doesn't want the dog on the couch, it is unfair for Son to let him up when she is not looking. It is the dog who will get yelled at when Mom catches him on the couch. Moreover, the dog now doesn't know if the couch is really off limits.

Consistency with commands is also important. The person doing the regular training should help everyone else who interacts with the dog to understand what the exact words are and how they are used. For example, "sit" and "down" are two different commands. "Sitdown" is not a command and would confuse the dog.

The most important response for you and your dog is for him to learn to come when called. To insure that every family member will get that response, regardless of who trained the dog, we have included "Whistle Training Your Dog."

How Often and How Long to Train

Individual dogs, like people, have different rates of learning. There is no formula for how long it will take your dog to be trained, so the practice plans in the following chapters are goal oriented—you practice as long as necessary to reach the week's goal.

The amount of time required for each exercise depends on your dog and on his breed. These lessons are designed to take approximately 20 to 30 minutes of practice per day. Two or three brief sessions, especially in the case of young puppies who have a shorter attention span, are preferable to one long one. Regardless of how many times a day you train, allow the dog to rest at least three hours between each session.

At the conclusion of each chapter there is a *Lesson Checklist* describing the goals and practice exercises for the week. Spend six days on each lesson before progressing to the next one. If you are having difficulty with one exercise, continue to work on it until you have reached the prescribed goal. Each lesson lays the foundation for the next one, so you cannot progress until your dog has reached the required level of proficiency.

You should practice every day. If you miss several consecutive days of training, start the current lesson from the beginning. For example, if you have completed two days of Lesson Five and miss a few days, repeat the first two days of Lesson Five before continuing with the remainder of that lesson.

When to Train

The time of day that you train can have a direct bearing on how quickly your dog learns. Since dogs are creatures of habit, much the way people are, train at approximately the same time each day, and it won't be long before your dog is telling *you* when it is time to train. This will become a special time set aside for you and your dog—one that is pleasurable for both of you.

While it is important to train regularly, every day if possible, it is also important that you feel positive about working with your dog. If you are in a bad mood, it is better to lose a day's training rather than take a chance on losing your temper. Your anger might set your training back far more than the loss of one day would.

Where to Train

During the initial training, practice in an area that is familiar to your dog and as free from distractions as possible. This allows your dog to learn in a location where you are the center of his attention. In later lessons, you will be instructed to take your dog to new areas so he learns that he must listen to you wherever he is.

How to End the Lesson

End each training lesson with a short play session that is fun for your dog. Do this on leash so that, even in play, you maintain physical control of your dog. Throw a ball or a stick. In the case of a dog who is not interested in retrieving, let him chase you around the yard, play with and pet your dog, but do not wrestle or roughhouse. Don't encourage conduct you find undesirable.

What to Wear

Wear comfortable clothes that neither interfere with your freedom of movement nor act as a distraction to your dog. Avoid skirts that are at his eye level, floppy sandals or heavy boots.

Smoking, Drinking and Medications

Do not smoke or carry a lighted cigarette, cigar or pipe while training—a hot ash can injure your dog's eyes.

Do not train your dog if you have had a cocktail or two—it will change your reaction time and your manner of speech in giving commands and praise. This difference may not be noticeable to you, but it might be just enough to confuse your dog and to impede the training process.

If you are on medication that affects your timing or makes you drowsy or nervous, don't train your dog.

COMMUNICATION:

Voice, Body Posture and Facial Expression

In the initial stages of training, the words you use are a foreign language to your dog. Because he doesn't understand the words, it is important that your tone of voice convey your meaning. When you are happy, your voice should be light and cheery. When you are giving a command, the tone of voice should be firm and friendly—never threatening or angry. When you wish to stop your dog from doing something, a sharp "STOP IT!" or "AH, AH!" gets the point across.

In addition to your tone of voice, your body posture and facial expression communicate your feelings to your dog. If you scowl, put your hands on your hips, or lean over your dog, he may be intimidated no matter what you say or how pleasantly you say it.

Commands are given in a quiet, pleasant tone of voice. A dog's hearing is very acute and there is no need to shout. Don't yield to the temptation to substitute yelling at your dog for proper training. Besides, if you bellow at your dog during normal circumstances, you have nothing left for emergencies.

Praise

The praise word used throughout the lessons, and for the remainder of your dog's life, is the single word "good," said with a smile and in a happy tone of voice. It must be sincere to be meaningful, and it is his reward for doing a job correctly.

Timing of praise is critical. It should follow the desired response as quickly as is humanly possible—almost simultaneously. **Praise delayed is praise denied.**

Petting

In the following lessons, particularly during the first four, you will be instructed not to pet your dog during the training session. You are not to pet your dog as a means of praise unless specifically instructed to do so.

Petting as a means of praise distracts your dog from the lesson to be learned, and if he breaks position while you pet him, you are unintentionally training him to break. This does not mean, of course, that you cannot pet your dog anytime you are not training him.

Nagging

Avoid nagging your dog by continuously repeating a command. If you habitually repeat "sitsitsitsitsit," you are training your dog to respond only to multiple commands. The command is "sit," period.

Also avoid chattering at your dog in the form of a conversation such as, "Sit Poopsie . . . Come on now . . . You know how to do this . . . Sit down Sweetie . . . That's a good girl . . . you can do it . . . sitsitsit." After all this, Poopsie is still standing, having completely tuned out her over-talkative owner.

One "sit" is all the dog should hear before being made to sit. In that way, the dog will be trained to respond to the first command.

An equally insidious practice is to engage in a prolonged tirade after your dog has done something you consider objectionable. Unless you catch your dog in the act, it is too late for any effective remedial action. Reproaches such as "What a bad boy you were! How many times do I have to tell you not to do that! Shame, shame, shame. I am very disappointed in you!" will only sour your relationship with your dog. Remember the example of the steak Konrad stole. Konrad thoroughly enjoyed the steak and could never understand why you were mad at him.

Avoid using your dog's name as a reprimand. Saying and repeating "Konra-a-a-d!" in a menacing tone creates an unpleasant association with his name which we obviously do not want. If you want him to stop something, say "Stop it!" If you want him to come, say "Come." Give clear instructions and commands rather than using his name in a negative manner.

Patience

Always be patient. With perserverance and praise you will succeed.

Learning Plateaus

It generally takes the dog about 35-42 days to commit to memory what you are teaching. For example, you begin teaching the sit on day one, Lesson 1. The learning process will be completed six weeks later, or by Lesson 7. Teaching the dog to stay is introduced in Lesson 2, and the learning process will be completed by Lesson 8.

The completion of learning is usually preceded by a learning plateau, during which the dog will give the appearance of having forgotten what he has learned. For example, during the sixth week of training, Lesson 6, the dog, who up to now has been advancing quickly, will seem to have forgotten everything you've taught him. Be prepared for this plateau, or you will be frustrated and discouraged. Continue training, mustering all the patience you can, but don't expect too much from your dog for the next few days. Once beyond the plateau, he will be better than ever.

Grooming

All dogs require occasional grooming to keep them in the best condition. If your dog's toenails are too long, it will be uncomfortable for him to walk. Ask your veterinarian or groomer to show you how to trim his nails. **If you can hear him coming, his nails are too long.** Similarly, excess hair around the feet and between the toes and pads should be trimmed for proper traction and comfort.

Keeping your dog's ears clean is important to his overall health. Ear infections can upset your dog's sense of balance, and can be quite painful. Once a week, check your dog's ears. If you detect an unusual odor, or see a dark discharge, consult your veterinarian. Long-haired, flop-eared dogs, such as spaniels and poodles, are prime candidates for ear infections.

All dogs require brushing but, if your dog has long hair, he will require more frequent brushing and combing than a short-haired dog to keep his hair free of mats. Matted hair is uncomfortable to the dog, and this discomfort will interfere with his training.

Dogs with hair over their eyes, who bump into furniture and appear disoriented, probably can't see through their hair. This will interfere with training, so you should trim the hair or tie it back. The belief that the sun will injure a dog's eyes is an old wives' tale.

Feeding and Exercise

Your dog's mind will not be fully alert if he has just eaten a big meal, so don't train him for two hours after feeding.

On the other hand, don't train him on an empty stomach. Give him a small snack to settle him down and the remainder of his meal after you have finished. Allow your dog a 20-minute rest after training before you feed him.

Be sure to give your dog a chance to relieve himself before you train him. He will not be able to concentrate on his lesson if he has to go to the bathroom.

Vocabulary

Your dog can learn an extensive vocabulary if you use the words consistently. The following list contains some suggestions for common situations. Familiarize yourself and your family with these words, and make sure that everyone uses the same words in the same context. Don't limit yourself to just this list, and don't hesitate to change a word if your dog already understands its meaning by another name. The word itself is not important. What is important is consistency. Those words with an asterisk next to them will be used in the training lessons; the others are used daily by most people:

AH, AH: Bark like. See *Stop it.*

*COME: Come to me. Response must always be rewarded.

DON'T JUMP: Don't jump on me or another person. Not to be confused with *Down.*

*DOWN: Lie down. If you've already used *Down* to mean *Don't Jump,* substitute another word for this. Perhaps *Drop.*

ENOUGH or NO MORE: "I don't want to play anymore" or "I don't want to pet you now."

*GIVE, OUT, DROP IT, or THANK YOU: To release to your hand an object held in the mouth.

*GOOD: Praise word, to be used frequently and with a happy voice.

*HEEL: To stay at your left side when walking, and to move to your left side and sit when not in motion.

IN, HUP, or GET IN: To get into the car or jump on the grooming table.

LET'S GO: To begin a walk, not at heel position.

MOVE: Get out of the way. For a dog in front of doors or cabinets.

OFF: Get off the furniture or people. Not to be confused with *Down.*

*OKAY or FREE: Release word, meaning "You can move now."

*SIT: Assume a sitting position.

*STAND: Assume a standing position and remain still.

*STAY: Remain in place.

STOP IT or STOP: Stop what you are doing instantly.

*TAKE IT: Retrieve an object and hold it.

WAIT: Different from *Stay;* meaning remain in the same general vicinity, but small movement is permitted. Useful when getting out of cars or going through doors.

Leash Training

Before beginning the training program, your dog must be familiar with and unafraid of the leash. If you have never had a leash on your dog or puppy before, or if your dog has had a prior bad experience with a leash and is afraid of it, the following schedule of introduction will familiarize him with the leash in a non-traumatic, pleasant manner. Because the leash will come to represent training to the dog, you must take care that it does not become a frightening tether.

Step 1: Place a buckle collar on your dog or puppy until he becomes used to it. Allow him a few days to become used to the collar.

Step 2: Attach a lightweight cloth or leather leash, or a piece of lightweight cord about twice the length of your dog to its collar, and let your dog drag it around. Keep an eye on him to make sure the leash doesn't wrap around a chair leg or a tree. Don't leave it on when you aren't supervising.

Step 3: Once your dog is ignoring the line or leash, pick up the end and hold it. Do not apply any pressure at this point. Follow your dog keeping the line slack. Work for a total of ten minutes on this.

Step 4: After your dog is used to being on the end of the leash while you hold it, the final step is for you to coax him in the direction you wish to go. Do not allow the leash to tighten without immediately loosening up again, and tell your pup how well he is doing when he is walking with you.

You cannot start training while your dog still fears the leash. Don't worry, most dogs readily take to the leash. Far from being intimidated by it, they are more likely to make it a pulling contest.

Equipment

The equipment used in training is very important. Attempting to train with inappropriate or ill-fitting equipment will make your effort more difficult or sometimes impossible.

Long Line

For some exercises you may need a 20 foot Long Line. This can be purchased or made from nylon cord available at hardware stores.

Dumbbell

A dumbbell is used to teach your dog to retrieve. A source of good dumbbells is J and J Dog Supplies, Inc., P.O. Box 1499, Galesburg, Illinois 61401.

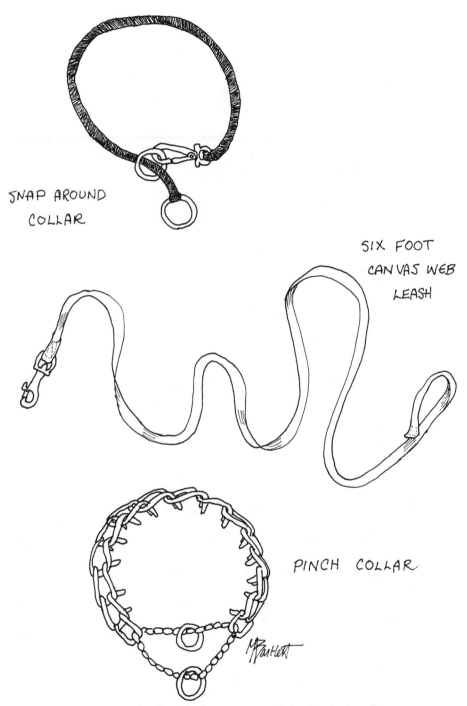

SNAP AROUND
COLLAR

SIX FOOT
CANVAS WEB
LEASH

PINCH COLLAR

Snap around collar, six foot canvas web leash, pinch collar.

Whistle

For whistle training.

The Collar

We use and recommend two types of collars: a nylon snap-around training collar and a pinch collar. Both collars are available at better pet stores. The soft nylon collar, not preferred, comes in one inch increments. The hard nylon comes in 1/2 inch increments and is available from Handcraft Collars, 3517 Victoria Road, Birmingham, Alabama 35223. When training a young puppy, be prepared to invest in more than one collar as your dog grows.

The pinch collar is adjustable and is available for small, medium and large dogs.

The Leash

Select a training leash of appropriate size for your dog. A toy dog on a one inch training leash with a huge bolt snap will quickly become exhausted from carrying around all that extra weight. On the other hand, attempting to train a St. Bernard on a string leash will be a frustrating and expensive proposition as the leash will break frequently.

The best leash for training is made of cotton web, six feet in length, and the appropriate width, with the proper-size snap for your individual dog. These leashes are washable and do not chafe your hands with rough edges. A suitable, quality leash is available from Handcraft Collars, address above.

A chain leash is an absolute no-no. A leather leash is acceptable but, again, it should be of the width and weight suitable for your dog.

How the Collar Works

In conjunction with your voice commands and physical placement of him, you communicate to your dog through the collar and leash. The collar check, a quick snap on the leash with an immediate release, teaches him where his advantage lies. The purpose of the check is to provide the dog with the motivation to move himself from Point A to Point B; it is not for you to physically pull or drag the dog from Point A to Point B. If the dog does not feel the check, he will not respond. On the other hand, if he feels it too strongly, it will cause him to dislike and fear training.

In addition to using the proper collar for your individual dog, the placement of the collar on the neck will affect his response. The closer to the shoulder area, the greater the muscle density. Even an extremely sensitive dog will feel little if anything if the collar sits very far down on the neck over these dense muscles. For most dogs, proper placement of the collar is high

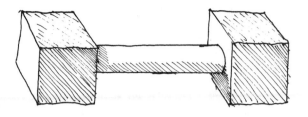

WOODEN DUMBBELL

WHISTLE

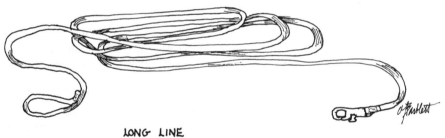

LONG LINE

Wooden dumbbell, whistle, long line.

up on the neck, just below the ears.

How to Measure for a Collar

To measure your dog for a proper fit, place a tape measure where the collar will go, and pull it snug. Collars come in 1/2 inch sizes, so you can get an exact fit for the neck measurement of your dog. If your dog has a thick ruff or a lot of hair around his neck, be sure to get the tape measure under the coat before reading the measurement. The collar will sit under the coat, so the measurement should be as close to the skin as possible.

When you are putting on the collar, your dog will flex his neck muscles much the way a horse will expand its girth when being saddled. Consequently, the collar will seem quite tight, and may be somewhat difficult to put on. Once your dog relaxes his neck muscles, the collar will have just the right amount of slack. With his muscles relaxed, there should be enough slack for you to get one finger under the collar of a small dog and two fingers under the collar of a large dog.

Extremes of Sensitivity

If your dog is extremely sensitive to touch, measure the collar to be placed at the mid point of the neck approximately half way between the ears and the shoulders, and begin your training on the non-action, or "dead", ring of the collar so that it does not tighten when you check your dog.

At the other extreme, the physically insensitive dog does not feel the collar the way most dogs do. In that case, we recommend that you purchase a pinch collar of suitable weight for your dog. The action of this type of collar is usually sufficient to get through to the dog who does not easily feel your check.

If there is a question in your mind as to which collar to use, begin with the assumption that your dog is medium sensitive, and then, if you feel you are not getting the proper response, you can go to the pinch collar.

How to Put on the Collar

The snap-around collar consists of a *loose ring,* a *stationary ring* and a *clasp.*

1.   Facing your dog, hold both rings of the collar in your right hand, and the clasp in your left.

2.   Place the collar under the dog's neck, and bring the ends up to the top of the dog's neck.

3.   Attach the clasp to the *loose* ring. The smooth side of the clasp should be next to the dog's skin so that the hook part of the clasp will not hurt him.

66

Select equipment of appropriate size for your dog...

Select equipment of appropriate size for your dog.

CORRECT PLACEMENT OF COLLAR FOR MOST DOGS

INCORRECT PLACEMENT, TOO LOW

Placement of the collar.

1.

2.

LOOSE
RING

3.

LEASH   STATIONARY RING

4.

MBartlett

How to put on a training collar.

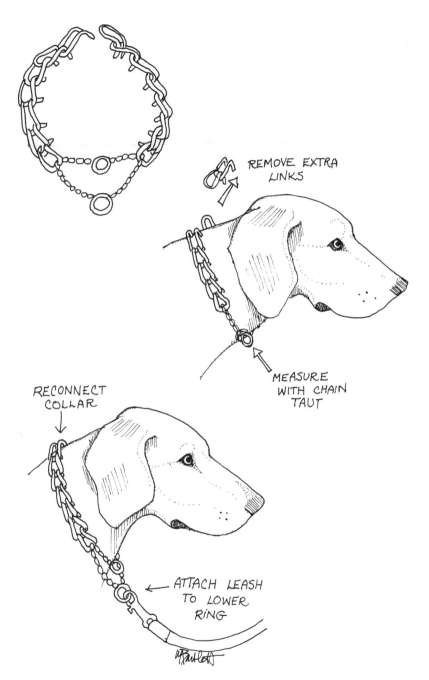

REMOVE EXTRA LINKS

MEASURE WITH CHAIN TAUT

RECONNECT COLLAR

ATTACH LEASH TO LOWER RING

How to put on a pinch collar.

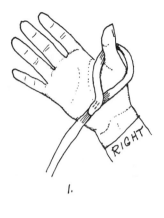

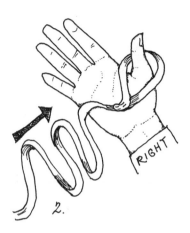

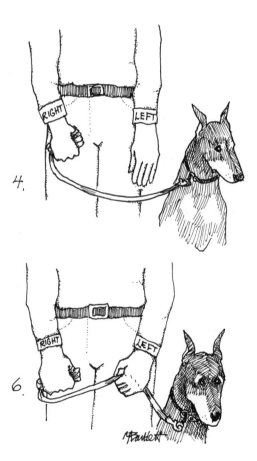

How to hold the leash.

Control Position.

4. The leash is attached to the *stationary* ring of the collar. **Do not leave this or any training collar on your dog when he is not being trained.**

The pinch collar consists of *removable links* and a *chain* with two *rings*. To put the pinch collar on your dog:

1. Separate two links approximately in the middle of the collar.
2. Remove extra links so that the collar fits snugly.
3. Place the collar around your dog's neck so that the chain is under his neck.
4. Connect the links at the back of the dog's neck.
5. Attach the leash to the outer ring of the chain.

How to Hold the Leash

1. Put your right thumb through the loop of the leash.
2. Fold the excess leash back and forth, accordion style, into your right hand. Be sure the part of the leash attached to the dog's collar comes out from under your little finger. Tighten your right hand into a fist around the leash.
3. Place your right hand against the front of your right leg, palm toward your leg.
4. With your left hand, grasp the leash in front of your left leg, palm facing down.
5. Keep both hands below your waist at all times, and keep your elbows straight and close to your sides.

From now on this will be referred to as *Control Position*. Practice leash handling with both hands until you are comfortable and proficient in its use.

Handler Adaptations

In the beginning of the training, many of the exercises require you to kneel on the floor next to your dog. If this posture is difficult or impossible for you, there are alternatives. You can sit in a chair or, if your dog is small, train him on a table initially.

How to Follow the Lessons

In the following lessons, each exercise contains three sections: 1) The *Object* of the exercise; 2) *Instructions* on how to perform it; and 3) A section entitled *Watch For*.

If you are having difficulty with an exercise, carefully review the instructions and evaluate exactly what you are doing. It may be that through some incorrect action you are inadvertently creating the difficulty. If necessary, have a friend or family member read the instructions and then watch you perform the exercise. You may not be aware of what you are do-

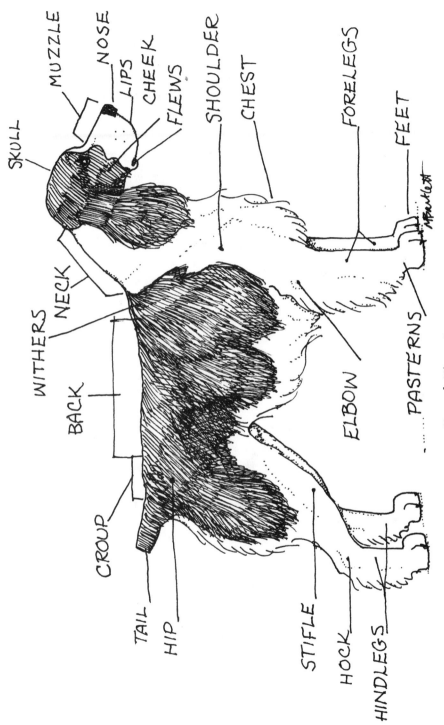

SKULL
MUZZLE
NOSE
LIPS
CHEEK
FLEWS
SHOULDER
CHEST
FORELEGS
FEET
WITHERS
NECK
BACK
CROUP
TAIL
HIP
ELBOW
PASTERNS
STIFLE
HOCK
HINDLEGS

Konrad. His anatomy.

ing wrong, but an observer can see it right away.

In general, **if your actions are correct, the dog's response will be correct.** Therefore, before getting angry with your dog or maligning his intelligence, be certain that it is not you who are at fault.

Instructions are quite precise. During your training you may be tempted to accept less than perfect responses on the part of your dog. You should be aware, however, that the degree of precision with which your dog responds to your training ultimately determines the amount of control you will have.

At the end of each chapter is a *Lesson Checklist*. This is a brief review of each exercise and your weekly goals. Review this checklist before beginning each training session. It will refresh your memory and remind you of exactly what exercises you have to practice that day.

4

Lesson 1

B<small>EFORE</small> BEGINNING THE LESSON, put the leash and collar on your dog as described in Chapter 3, "Getting Ready." Read through all the instructions completely. Before trying it with your dog, reread the instructions, and study the illustrations. Then perform the exercise with your dog. After doing it once, re-read the instructions to double check the sequence of command, action, and praise, and then repeat the exercise.

We refer to the dog as "Konrad;" you will use your own dog's name.

Giving a demonstration in front of a class, we used an imaginary dog, and gave the command, "Fido, Heel." Instructing the class to now perform as demonstrated, Barbara turned to her German Shepherd, Max, and said, "Fido, Heel."

So whenever the instructions say "Konrad, Heel," you substitute the name of your dog for "Konrad."

Sit—Sequence 1

Object: To teach you to physically place your dog in the sitting position.

Instructions: Have your dog standing at your left side, facing in the same direction you are. Place your right hand against your dog's chest, in front of his forelegs. If your dog is bouncy, position your right hand in his collar at the back of his neck.

Place your left hand on your dog's withers. Stroke lightly down the entire length of your dog's back, over the tail and tuck him into a sitting position by applying equal pressure behind the stifles and against the chest. As you begin applying pressure, say "sit." Do *not* use your dog's name.

Placing your dog

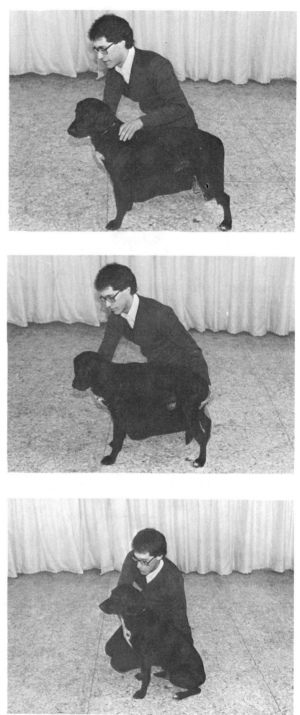

into

a sit.

Placing your dog

into a stand.

Your dog will sit on your left hand while your right hand prevents him from moving. Hold him in this position for five seconds while you *verbally* praise him for sitting. Do not pet your dog at this time. Repeat this five times, in conjunction with the Stand.

Watch for: Be sure that your right hand is on the chest or in the collar, not on the throat, and that your left hand starts at the withers. The action is a tucking one, not applying pressure until you begin tucking in behind the stifles. The pressure with your left hand is *forward* not *downward.* Remember to use the command "sit," without his name at this time, as you tuck the dog into position. Your dog may sit on your hand. This will remind you not to pet the dog as you praise.

Stand—Sequence 1

Object: To teach the dog to stand still.

Instructions: Kneel beside the sitting dog as you were for the sit, with the dog facing in the same direction you are.

To position your dog in a stand, place two fingers of your right hand in the collar, under the dog's muzzle, so that your palm is toward the floor and the back of your hand is under the dog's chin. Place the back of your left hand, palm facing forward, in front of your dog's stifles. With your right hand, pull forward, *parallel to the ground,* guiding your dog into a stand, saying "stand." Again, do not use his name. Your left hand in front of the stifles prevents the dog from moving forward or sitting. As you *hold* your dog in the standing position, praise with "good." Hold your dog in a stand for ten seconds before you sit him.

Goal/Assignment: Work on a one-minute stand this week, with your dog standing still.

Watch for: Be sure your movement with your right hand is parallel to the floor, not pulling upward. An upward motion would make it very difficult for the dog to stand. Keep the palm of your left hand facing forward. Do not pet your dog during this exercise, as this will cause him to move.

Down—Sequence 1

Object: To teach you to physically place your dog in the down position.

Instructions: Kneel beside the sitting dog facing the same direction as you are, and position your hands as follows. Your right hand, palm facing upward, is placed behind the dog's right foreleg, just below the elbow. Drape your left arm across your dog's withers, so that your left hand, palm upward, is behind your dog's left foreleg, just below the elbow. Keep your

78

Hand position for placing a dog into a down.

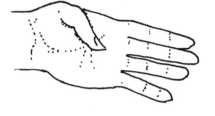

FOLD THUMBS IN

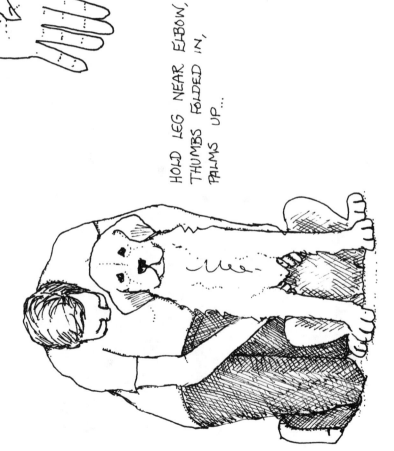

HOLD LEG NEAR ELBOW,
THUMBS FOLDED IN,
PALMS UP...

Placing a puppy

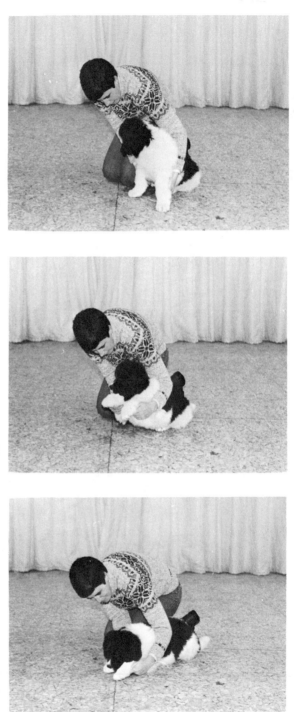

into

a down.

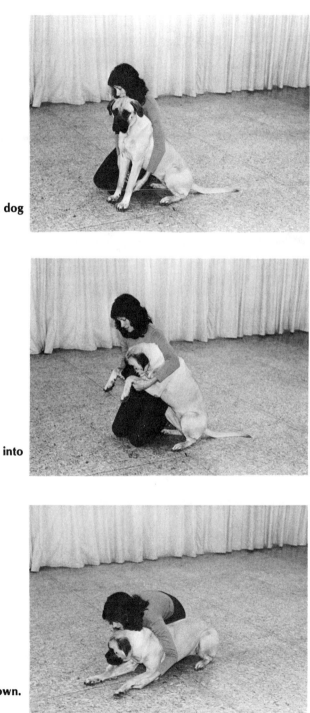

Placing an adult dog

into

a down.

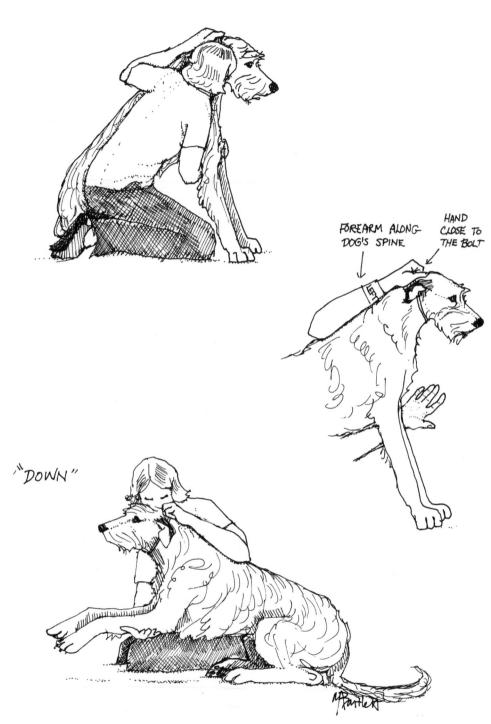

FOREARM ALONG DOG'S SPINE

HAND CLOSE TO THE BOLT

"DOWN"

Alternate technique for the down.

palms open, thumbs in your palms. Lift the dog's forelegs up, and then lower them to the ground with "down." You may have to apply downward pressure on the dog's withers with your left forearm. Hold the dog in the down position while you praise. Do not pet your dog or use his name.

To repeat this exercise, first place your dog in a sit from a down by saying "sit" as you raise the front end by lifting with your right hand on his chest, or pulling up with your hand in the collar at the back of his neck.

Watch for: Many dogs object to having pressure applied to their forelegs. This can cause such problems as fidgeting, pulling away, or even protest biting, so be sure you are not applying pressure to the dog's legs with your thumbs or fingers: your palms should be open with your thumbs in your palms as you place the dog in the down position.

Don't pull the dog's legs out from under him, as this may frighten him; it may also cause him to lift up his rear as you are pulling on the front. Lift before you lower, and the dog cannot raise his rear.

Be sure your hands are just below the elbow and not farther down on the leg. This gives you the necessary leverage to lift him into the down position.

If your dog has had a previously unpleasant experience having his legs touched, you may have to spend some time doing a little remedial work before beginning this exercise. Have your dog sit at your side and cradle his right foreleg on the palm of your right hand. Talk to the dog as you lightly bounce his leg on your hand. **Be sure you do not apply pressure to the top of the leg.** Repeat with the left leg in your left hand. When the dog has relaxed in this position, place him into the down.

Alternate Technique: If your dog is too tall for you to reach across his back with your left arm, you can use the following alternate technique. Bring the rings of the collar to the back of the dog's neck, kneel next to your dog with him sitting at your left side. Fold the leash into your left hand and grasp the bolt snap close to the collar. Place your left forearm along the dog's spine. Your right hand and forearm go behind both of the dog's front legs, with your palm facing away from the dog. Lift or slide the front legs up and then lower the dog to the ground, saying "down." Praise.

Heel Position

Your dog is in heel position when he is facing in the same direction you are and is lined up next to you on your left side, with the area between his head and shoulder in line with your left hip. He should be close to your left leg, but should not be crowding you or interfering with your movement. Heel position remains the same whether your dog is sitting, standing, lying down, or moving at your side. The next few exercises help to teach the dog to understand heel position.

Use of Name with Heel Command

For all heeling exercises, use your dog's name before the command. The use of the dog's name will signify that you are about to move and want him to move.

Right-Turn in Place—Sequence 1

Object: A 90° turn to the right away from your dog. An exercise to teach him heel position.

Instructions: Place your dog in a sit at your left side in heel position. Place the rings of the collar under the dog's chin. Hold the leash as instructed. Place your left hand on the leash directly above the snap and keep both hands close together in front of your legs. If you have a small dog, bend your knees, not your torso.

Place your right foot at a 90° angle, one large step to the right. With "Konrad, Heel," bring your left foot together with your right. Place your dog into a sit in heel position by crouching as you place your right hand against the chest and tuck with your left hand. Praise.

Goal/Assignment: Repeat five times.

Watch for: Be sure your left hand is close to the snap. **The farther away from the snap you position your left hand on the leash, the less control you have of your dog.** If your leash has two feet of slack, your dog may end up two feet away before you can get a hand on his chest to sit him.

Be sure that you place your right foot before giving the command. The motion of your left leg will cause your dog to make the turn. If he doesn't, guide him with the leash.

When you crouch to place your dog into a sit, do not hover over his back, but bend your knees and slightly rotate your upper body toward him to sit him. He should be facing straight ahead, in line with your left thigh.

The right hand against his chest will stop his forward motion and enable you to sit him exactly in heel position.

About Turn in Place—Sequence 1

Object: A 180° turn to the right away from your dog and another way of teaching him heel position.

Instructions: Your posture, your dog's position and that of the leash and collar are the same for this exercise as for the Right-Turn In Place. To execute the About-Turn In Place, say "Konrad, Heel," and take two steps straight forward. Turn in place 180°, away from your dog, and take two steps straight forward again. Place your dog in a sit with the command "sit" followed by praise.

84

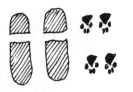

"KONRAD, HEEL"

**Diagram for the
Right-Turn in Place.**

Right-Turn

in Place.

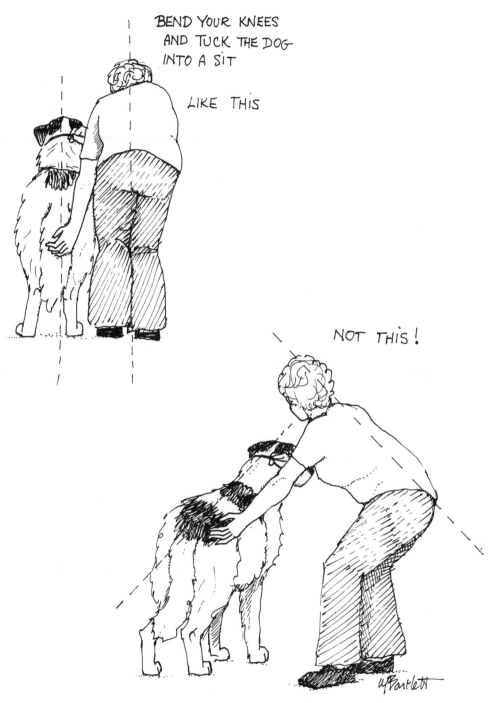

Correct and incorrect body positions for the Turns in Place.

Goal/Assignment: Execute five of each of these turns per session.

Watch for: Be sure that you take two steps straight forward before you turn in place away from your dog, and then take another two steps straight forward after you have completed the turn. If you simply take two steps forward, turn, stop and sit your dog, this will not give your dog a chance to move completely around the turn and straighten out again. When you sit your dog, he should be lined up exactly as for the Right-Turn In Place.

Heeling, Straight Line

Object: To teach your dog to walk by your side in heel position, on a loose leash, and without pulling, forging ahead or lagging behind.

Instructions: To begin this exercise, sit your dog in heel position. Take the full length of your leash and throw it over your right shoulder, so it is across your chest. If you are tall, or if you have a very short dog, tuck the leash through a belt loop on the right side of your pants.

Once you begin walking, you are to keep your hands off the leash at all times unless your dog strays from heel position. If your dog does get out of heel position, grasp the leash in your *left* hand, quickly check the dog back to your left side, and *immediately* remove your hand from the leash. Act as if the leash is hot—very hot—and touching it hurts.

Your command to your dog, before you begin walking, is "Konrad, Heel," in a pleasant voice. Once you have started walking, you should say nothing to your dog except to praise him when he is in heel position. If he is out of heel position, do not say anything. Simply check him back with your left hand, and follow with immediate praise. Do not pet your dog during this exercise.

Goal/Assignment: Practice this week until you can heel your dog for ten paces in a straight line without having to check him.

Watch for: Do not keep your hand on the leash to hold your dog in heel position. Bring the dog to heel position, praise and remove your hand immediately. Remember, the leash is very hot. Every time he leaves your side, check him.

The purpose of the check is to teach the dog where his advantage lies; that is, to remain in heel position. The check is a quick snap on the leash, with an immediate release. Pulling him, or physically restraining him with constant pressure, will teach him to pull—not to heel.

Keep your hands off your dog while moving; use verbal praise.

Check the dog with your left hand only.

The command "heel" is used only when you start; it is not repeated while you are walking. Repeating the command is nagging.

Be sure you are walking briskly, in order to keep his interest and attention on you. Walk as if you were in a hurry (e.g., late for an appointment).

About-Turn While Heeling

Object: To teach your dog to remain in heel position when you make a turn. As with the About-Turn In Place, this is a 180° turn to the right, away from your dog.

Instructions: To execute an About-Turn While Heeling, call your dog's name to get his attention; grasp the leash in your left hand; turn 180° in place, away from your dog, while guiding him around; and continue walking in the opposite direction. Throughout the turn, keep your feet together and maintain a brisk pace.

Watch for: Come out of the turn briskly and continue walking without waiting for your dog. If you stop, he will stop.

Leash Handling for Off-Leash Heeling
(The Slip Release)

Object: To teach you how to handle the leash, preparatory to off-leash heeling.

Instructions: Take the loop end of the leash, seam side down, and thread it under your dog's collar, toward his tail. Place the loop over your left thumb and grasp the leash lightly with the fingers of your left hand. Hold the clasp of the leash in your right hand and accordion fold the excess into your right hand. Assume Control Position. To release, drop the loop of the leash off your thumb and, without moving your left hand, draw the leash through the fingers of your left hand by folding it neatly into your right hand. Be sure to fold the entire leash into your right hand.

Practice this maneuver without your dog first. Use a chair back as if it were your dog's collar. Work on becoming proficient at performing the Slip Release before starting Lesson 2.

Goal/Assignment: Practice five times per session.

Watch for: Be sure to keep your left hand absolutely still. All motion is with your right hand, leash slipping through the left.

Long Down—Sequence 1

Object: To teach the dog that you are the pack leader.

Instructions: Begin by getting yourself settled comfortably on the floor. You will be there for one half hour, so be sure you have everything you will need during that time. If you want to watch TV or read, you may do so, but be aware of why you are there.

Sit on the floor with your dog, and place him in the down position, as above. Praise, but do not pet. After he is down, remove your hands. But be prepared to apply downward pressure with your left hand at the withers every time he wants to get up in order to prevent him from rising. As you apply pressure, repeat the command and remove your hand. Repeat as often as necessary. If your dog actually does get up, replace him in the down as you did to begin the exercise. The "stay" command is not used for this exercise.

After 30 minutes, release your dog from the down. Your release word can be almost anything, but once you have decided on a word or phrase, be consistent in your use of it. Examples of release words are "Okay" or "Free." If your dog has fallen asleep, wake him up and then release him.

If something interrupts you during the Long Down, such as the telephone or someone coming to visit, and you must end the exercise, be sure to release the dog first. This exercise teaches the dog that you are in charge. If you don't release him, and he learns that he can get up on his own, the entire object of the exercise is lost.

Goal/Assignment: Repeat this exercise three times this week for 30 minutes each.

Watch for: Maintain an even temper during this exercise. If your dog gets up every five seconds for the entire 30 minutes, then you must put him down 360 times during the half hour. And, each time you replace him in position, your command should be given in the same tone of voice. Your 359th "down" should sound the same as your first.

Your dog should remain in position, or you should be replacing him, during the entire 30 minutes. He can move slightly—to scratch himself, to readjust his weight, or to move from one side to the other—as long as he remains lying down.

Do not yield to the temptation to keep a hand on your dog, as this will negate the purpose of the exercise. Also, this is not a play session, so don't let your dog play with a toy during the 30-minute down.

(Jane seemed to be having difficulty establishing her leadership over Adam. When asked if she were doing the Long Down, she said, "Yes. He loves them because he gets a new rawhide chewy every time.")

What Jane was doing was bribing the dog to remain in position. She was not establishing herself as pack leader. Once Jane did the exercise correctly, her training became successful.

LESSON CHECKLIST—Lesson 1

As you start working with your dog, keep in mind that **the degree of precision determines the amount of control.** If you are lackadaisical about how you expect your dog to respond, he in turn will be lackadaisical about how he responds.

Sit

With your dog at your left side, facing straight ahead, place your right hand against the dog's chest, and begin with your left hand at the withers. Say "sit" (no name) as you stroke down his back with your left hand, stroke over the tail, and tuck the dog into a sit by applying pressure behind the stifles. Praise by saying "good" while holding him in position. Do not pet your dog at this time. Repeat five times per session.

Down

Place your right hand behind your dog's right foreleg, palm open and facing away from your dog, thumb in palm. Reach across his back with your left arm, and place your left hand behind his left foreleg. Say "down" (no name) as you lift his front end and lower him to the ground. Praise when he is down. Do not pet your dog at this time.

Right Turn in Place

Sit your dog in heel position and gather the leash short in your right hand. Place your left hand close to the snap of the leash. Keep both hands in front of your legs and close together. Place your right foot at a 90° angle, one large step to the right. Say, "Konrad, heel," and bring your left foot together with your right. Say "sit" and place him in position. Praise. Practice five times per session.

About Turn in Place

Sit the dog in heel position and gather the leash short in your right hand. Place your left hand close to the snap of the leash. Keep both hands in front of your legs and close together. Say, "Konrad, heel;" take two steps straight forward; turn in place 180°, away from your dog, to face in the opposite direction; and take two more steps straight forward. Say "sit" and place the dog in a sit at your side. Praise. Practice five times per session.

Heeling

Throw the leash across your chest and over your right shoulder. Sit your dog in heel position. Call out, "Konrad, Heel," and begin walking at a brisk pace. When your dog strays from heel position, use your left hand to

1.

CHECK!

Leash over
the shoulder.

2.

"GOOD
DOG!"

3.

Heeling with leash over shoulder.

check him back to position, praise him immediately, and quickly take your hand off the leash. Practice until you can heel for ten paces in a straight line without checking your dog.

Stand

Place two fingers of your right hand in the dog's collar under the muzzle, palm toward the floor. Pull forward and parallel to the floor with your right hand as you tell the dog, "Stand . . . good." Use your left hand, palm forward, to apply pressure against the front of the stifles. Hold him in position as you praise. Do not pet the dog during this exercise. Have your dog stand still without fidgeting for one minute, once each session. Remain on your knees with your hands in position for the entire minute.

Slip Release Leash Handling

Practice this five times a session, or until you are comfortable with it. You should be able to execute the release without moving your left hand, and without thinking about the mechanics involved. Practice without your dog.

Long Down

Sit on the floor beside your dog, place him in the down position using the command "down," and remain there with him and keep him in the down position for 30 minutes. At the end of the 30 minutes, release him. Practice three times this week.

If your dog seems reluctant or resentful about doing the Stand, the Down, or both, you should not do both exercises during the same session. Moreover, you should alter his outlook with extra rewards, such as doing one or the other in conjunction with his dinner. For example, if your dog has difficulty accepting standing still, fix his dinner and put it on the counter. Then practice with him for several minutes, making sure he is successful, and then feed him as a reward. You will find that after several days of this regimen, your dog will have a much-improved view of standing still.

1

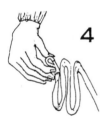

2

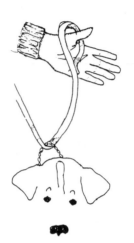

3

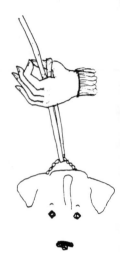

4

5

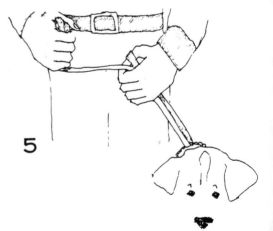

The Slip

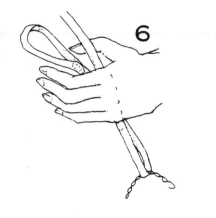

6

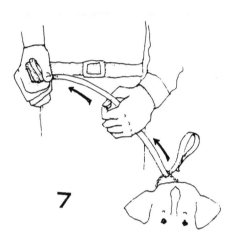

7

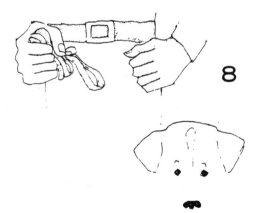

8

Release.

5

Lesson 2

Sit—Sequence 2

Object: To teach the dog to respond to the command "sit."

Instructions: Select an object of interest to your dog—a ball or squeaky toy. If your dog is not interested in toys, use a small food treat. Depending on the size of your dog, kneel or stand next to him. He should be standing at your left side facing in the same direction you are. Hold the object in your right hand, just in front of your dog's nose. Motion with the object at a 45° angle upward from in front of your dog's nose to a point directly over his head, slightly behind his eyes. Make the motion quickly as you say "sit." Your dog will raise his head to see the object, causing his rear end to drop into a sitting position. Praise and let him have the object briefly, but don't pet. If your dog does not sit on command, place him in a sit as you have been for the past week, let him have the object and try it again.

Goal/Assignment: Practice this five times per session.

Watch for: Always say "sit" in conjunction with the motion of your hand holding the object. The purpose of this exercise is to teach your dog to respond to the verbal command, so you must say it every time you make the motion with the object. If your dog is jumping up to grab the object, you are holding it too far above his head. If you are holding the object properly and your dog is still jumping up, put your left hand in his collar at the back of his neck to steady him in position and prevent him from jumping up.

Down—Sequence 2

Object: To teach your dog to lie down in response to your verbal command.

96

Sit with object of attraction.

Down from side

with object

of attraction.

Instructions: Kneel next to your dog and sit him at your left side, facing in the same direction you are. Place your left hand on the dog's withers to prevent him from getting up. Hold the object in your right hand, at a starting point just above the dog's eye level, in front of his face. Motion with your right hand down to the floor and slightly away from in front of your dog — a rounded "L"-shaped motion. The object should be within your dog's reach when he is lying down. Make your motion quickly as you say "down." When he is down, your dog may have the object briefly. Praise but do not pet. If he fails to follow the object down, place him down as you did last week, give him the object and try it again.

Goal/Assignment: Practice five times in conjunction with the Sit.

Watch for: If your dog gets up to walk toward the object, you have not placed your left hand at the withers to prevent this. Under no circumstances push downward with your left hand, but simply hold it there to prevent your dog from getting up.

The object should not be so close to your dog's feet that he can reach it without lying down, nor so far away that he cannot get it when he does lie down. Do not let your dog have the object until he is completely lying down.

Use the word "down" each time you make the motion with the object. The purpose of this exercise is to teach your dog to respond to the verbal command, so say it every time.

Give

Object: To teach your dog to relinquish any object in his mouth on command. Does not apply to treats, but definitely to chicken bones.

Instructions: After your dog has had the object briefly, say "Give" and remove it from his mouth. Immediately upon his release of the object, praise but don't pet.

Watch for: If your dog is reluctant to give you the object, place your left hand *under* the dog's jaw—fingers on one side, thumb on the other—at the back of his mouth near where his jaw hinges. Apply pressure to the lips against his teeth as you say "Give." As soon as the dog's mouth opens, *immediately* release your pressure, take the object, and praise.

Sit from a Down with Object

Object: To teach your dog to sit on command from a down.

Instructions: The motion with the object in front of your dog's face is the same as for the sit from the standing position. Place your left hand in the collar behind the dog's neck to guide him into a sit if necessary. Praise, but don't pet.

Stand—Sequence 2

Object: To steady your dog in the standing position.

Instructions: Your body posture and your dog's position should be the same as last week, with you kneeling on the floor beside your dog. After your dog is standing, do not touch him with your left hand in front of the stifles, provided he is steady and doesn't fidget. Continue to hold the collar with your right hand under the chin. Praise, but do not pet, when he is standing quietly.

Goal/Assignment: Keep your dog standing still for 2 minutes each session.

Watch for: If your dog is fidgeting or is unsteady, continue to hold him in position with your left hand as you did last week. Gradually try to wean him away from having your left hand touching him.

Right- and About-Turn in Place—Sequence 2

Object: This is the second progression for this exercise: teaching your dog to sit at heel.

Instructions: For the Right-Turn in Place, place the rings of the collar at the back of your dog's neck. Hold the leash short in both hands, as you have done for the last week. Position your right foot as before, say "Konrad, Heel" and follow with the left. Transfer the leash from your left hand to your right and grasp it close to the snap. Check with your right hand straight up, and tuck your dog into a sit with the left. Say "sit" and praise. Concentrate on keeping your body facing straight ahead, and having your dog sit absolutely straight facing the same direction in which you are facing.

For the About-Turn in Place, take two steps straight forward, turn in place, 180° away from your dog, to face in the opposite direction, and then take another two steps straight forward. Sit your dog as above.

Goal/Assignment: Repeat each turn in place five times per session.

Watch for: Be sure your right hand is checking straight upward and not pulling backward or toward you across your body. Backward pressure will cause your dog to sit behind you, and he will not be in correct position by your side. Drawing him toward you will cause him to sit crooked.

Grasp the leash with your right hand very close to the snap so that you

100

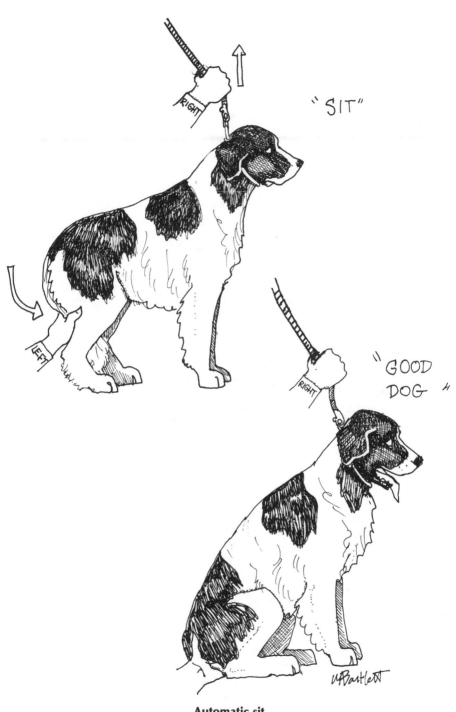

Automatic sit.

don't have any slack between your hand and the dog's collar. **The closer to the collar you position your right hand, the more control you have over your dog.**

Automatic Sit in Motion—Sequence 1

Object: To teach your dog to sit in heel position when you come to a stop.

Instructions: Throw the leash over your shoulder as you have done for Heeling. Say "Konrad, heel," take four or five steps forward, then come to a complete stop saying "sit." Place him into a sit as for the Turns in Place. Grasp the leash close to the snap with your right hand as you begin to come to a halt. This will stop your dog's forward motion and give you control as you tuck him into the sit. Don't forget your praise.

Goal/Assignment: Repeat five times per session.

Watch for: Be sure to keep your body facing straight ahead as you sit your dog. Do not turn toward your dog. Line him up with your left thigh as you crouch to tuck him into a sit. Your check should be straight up, not backward nor toward you.

Heeling with Leash over Shoulder

Instructions: Heel your dog in a straight line or, if space allows, a large counter circle. Keep your pace brisk, and treat the leash as if it has gotten even hotter. If your dog strays from heel position, check him back with your left hand, and take your hand off the leash. Praise immediately.

Goal/Assignment: Practice until you can heel your dog 15 paces and make two about turns without a check.

CIRCLES:

Object: To teach your dog to remain in heel position during changes in direction.

Circle Left

Instructions: Assume Control Position—leash held in both hands as described in Chapter 3—and make a complete circle to the left about four feet in diameter, with the command "Konrad, Heel," walking *very slowly*. After completing the circle, stop and sit your dog, transferring the leash from your left hand to your right, checking straight up with your right and tucking him into a sit with your left. Say "sit" and praise.

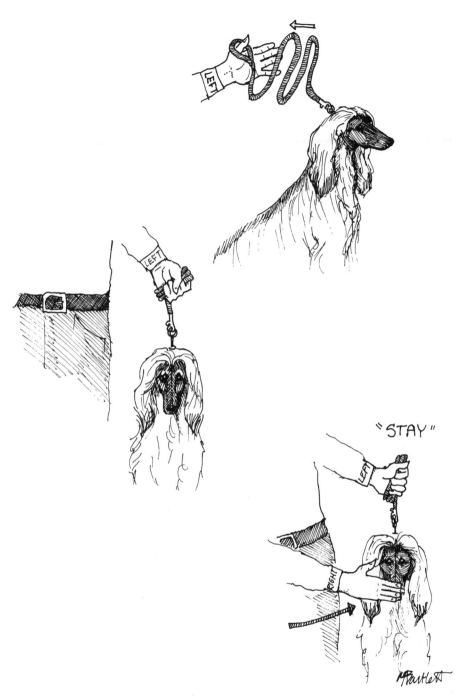

The stay hand signal.

Circle Right

Instructions: Assume Control Position, say, "Konrad, Heel," and make a complete circle about four feet in diameter to the right, trotting with small, choppy steps. After completing the circle, stop and sit your dog as above.

Goal/Assignment: Three of each circle per session.

Watch for: On Circles Right, make sure you are trotting and not running. Your dog should remain at your side.

On Circles Left your pace must slow way down as you keep your dog at heel.

Stay Hand Signal

To teach the Stay, use the hand signal as well as the voice command. The hand signal for Stay is given with the right hand, palm open toward your dog, brought across your body directly in front of your dog's nose in a sideways motion.

Sit-Stay—Sequence 1

Object: To teach your dog to remain in a sitting position on the command "Stay" and not to move until released.

Instructions: Place your dog in a sit at your left side. Bring the rings of the collar to the back of his neck, between his ears. Fold the leash short into your left hand. With your left hand, hold the leash taut, but not tight, above your dog's head, between his ears. Keep your left hand below your waist or, in the case of a tall dog, keep your hand close to the snap of the leash directly over your dog's head.

Maintaining slight tension on the leash, give the Stay hand signal and say "stay." Do not use his name. Pivot directly in front of your dog, count to 10 and pivot back next to him. Release the tension on the leash, pause briefly, then praise. He must remain in position while being praised. Then release him from the Stay with your release word.

Goal/Assignment: A 30-second Sit-Stay. Gradually increase your time from a *silent* count of 10 to a 30-second stay. When your dog has stayed to the count of 30 for 3 days in a row, further practice should be done with no tension on the leash.

Watch for: If your dog is rising up on his hind legs or is pawing at the leash, you have too much pressure on the collar.

Be sure that your hand signal comes across your body toward your dog from right to left, rather than in a hitting motion toward your dog which he might construe as a threat. Don't touch your dog's nose.

104

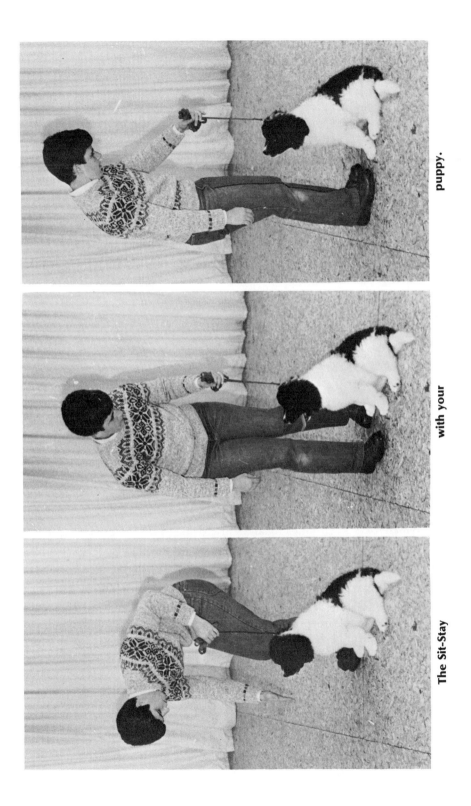

The Sit-Stay   with your   puppy.

Remain directly in front of your dog this week. Your feet and his feet should be practically touching. If you are further away than that, you don't have proper control with your leash. Stand erect, and don't hover over your dog.

If you need to replace your dog because he has moved, place him in exactly the same spot. Do it with a minimum of touching and talking. Any touching at this point may be interpreted by the dog as petting, and hence will act as a reward for having moved. To minimize this effect, replace him as quickly as possible using the leash and collar; tuck quickly into a sit if necessary; take your hands off immediately; and repeat the "stay" command.

When counting, do so silently.

Always be sure to pause between pivoting back to your dog's side, praising, and releasing him from the Stay. You don't want him to learn that your return means the end of the exercise, which is what will happen if you don't pause.

Off-Leash Heeling—Sequence 1

Object: To introduce your dog to Off-Leash Heeling.

Instructions: This exercise should be practiced in a safe area, where your dog will not be able to run away or into the road. Position your leash under the collar for the slip release. Sit your dog at your left side, and hold the leash in the slip-release position, ready to begin.

With "Konrad, heel," begin making a circle to the left at a very slow pace. As you enter the circle, release your dog by performing the slip release. After completing the circle, stop and place him into a sit by putting your right hand on his chest and tucking him into a sit with your left as you did last week. Say "sit." Praise but don't pet.

Goal/Assignment: One circle off-leash per training session.

Watch for: Keep your left hand still and don't yank the leash out from under the collar. Perform the slip release motion smoothly with your right hand, and be sure that the entire length of leash goes through your left hand and is neatly folded into your right hand.

There can be no tension on the leash before you release or the exercise will be unsuccessful. If your dog is pulling on the leash and you cannot get any slack to release, practice Heeling With Leash Over Shoulder until you have reached the goal of heeling with no tension on the leash for 10 paces. Then try the slip release for Off-Leash Heeling again.

Slip Surprise

What happens if Konrad, once off leash, bolts? Keeping in mind that

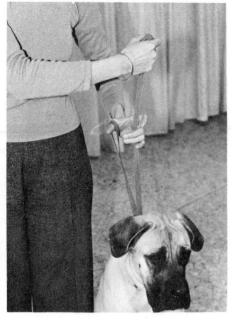

Preparing

for the

Slip

Release.

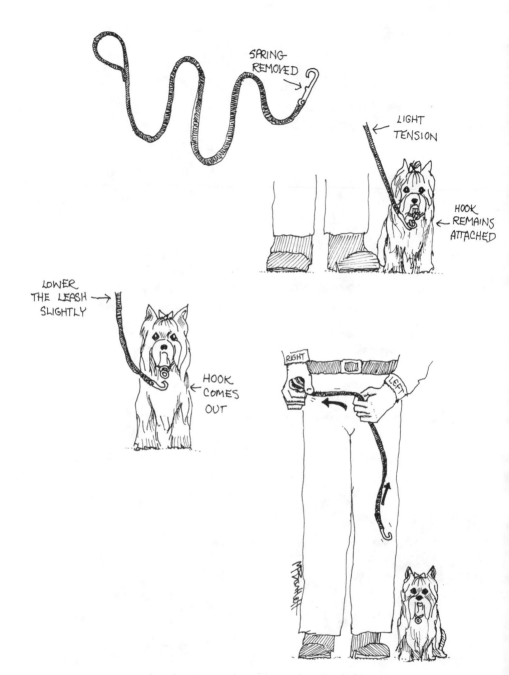

The alternate technique for the Slip Release.

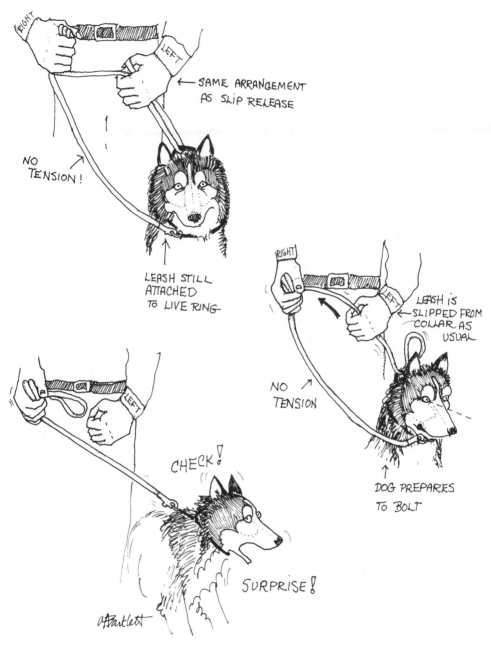

SAME ARRANGEMENT AS SLIP RELEASE

NO TENSION!

LEASH STILL ATTACHED TO LIVE RING

LEASH IS SLIPPED FROM COLLAR AS USUAL

NO TENSION

DOG PREPARES TO BOLT

CHECK!

SURPRISE!

The Slip Surprise.

your dog learns by repetition, you must avoid putting him in a position where he can bolt again. Begin the slip release again, but this time leave the snap attached to his training collar. Grasp the leash approximately in the middle with your right hand, and execute the release as before. Now when your dog bolts, as he surely will, let him go to the end of the leash and then firmly and emphatically check him—surprise!

Repeat this procedure three times, checking firmly each time, even if the dog no longer attempts to bolt. If after this procedure your dog is not performing the exercise, review your Heeling on Leash and examine whether your dog is responding to the check. You should also use the Slip Surprise technique as a matter of course if you are unable to practice Off-Leash Heeling in a safe area.

This particular exercise, Off-Leash Heeling, tells you whether or not your training is getting through to your dog. Repeated failures are indicative of incorrect collar position, incorrect collar (you may have to go to the pinch collar) or incorrect use of the check (you may be pulling on the leash and maintaining pressure instead of *snapping* with an immediate release, or your checks may not be firm enough).

Alternate Technique: For small dogs and dogs with excessive hair, the slip release is executed with a leash from which the spring has been removed from the snap so that all that remains is a hook similar to a fish hook.

With the rings of the collar under the dog's neck, hook the snap into the live ring of the collar so that it faces the dog. When you begin your circle, maintain a light tension on the leash so that the hook remains attached to the collar. To release, lower the leash so the hook comes out of the ring and gather the entire leash into your right hand through your left as for the slip release.

Long Sit—Sequence 1

Object: To teach your dog to sit still.

Instructions: Position yourself in a chair, and place your dog in a sit by your side, with the command "sit." He is to remain in position for 10 minutes. If at any time during the ten minutes your dog tries to get up or lie down, reposition him with "sit." At the end of this period, release your dog.

Goal/Assignment: Do this three times this week, 10 minutes each.

Long Down—Sequence 2

Object: The next progression of this exercise.

Instructions: You may sit in a chair this week with your dog lying down by your side. Be prepared to replace your dog if he gets up, or to prevent him from getting up just as you did last week. At the end of the 30 minutes, release your dog.

Goal/Assignment: Do this three times this week, 30 minutes each.

Watch for: If your dog still tries to get up repeatedly during the Long Down, you will have to do this exercise five times this week and, if necessary, sit on the floor as in Lesson 1.

Do the Long Sit and the Long Down on alternate days.

Whistle Training—Sequence 1

Object: This exercise teaches the dog to respond to a whistle—to stop what he is doing and return immediately to the person blowing the whistle. The first advantage to teaching this exercise is that the whistle carries farther than your voice. The second advantage is that the dog will respond to the whistle regardless of who is blowing it. This includes children to whom the dog might not otherwise come when called.

Instructions: Take your dog to a room with no distractions. Have treats in your pocket and the whistle around your neck. When your dog is paying no particular attention to you, blow the whistle—one short blast—and wait until your dog comes over to you to investigate. As soon as he does, give him a treat and praise. Repeat this sequence as soon as he is no longer paying any attention to you. The dog will learn to come to you when he hears the whistle because he is rewarded for doing so every time.

Goal/Assignment: Repeat this exercise until your dog makes the connection between the whistle and the reward. This will be apparent to you by your dog's eager response to the whistle blast. Thereafter, practice three to five times per session.

Watch for: If your dog is particularly sensitive to sounds, blow the whistle quietly.

The sound of the whistle should be the only stimulus that attracts your dog to you. Do not give any other commands or signals to try to attract your dog to come to you as that would defeat the object of this exercise.

LESSON CHECKLIST—Lesson 2

Sit—Sequence 2

With your dog standing at your left side, hold the object of attraction in your right hand. As you say "sit," bring your right hand quickly from in front of the dog's head, at nose level, to a point directly above his head, slightly behind his eyes. Praise when he sits. Give him the object. Repeat five times per session.

Down—Sequence 2

With your dog sitting at your left side, place your left hand on the withers, and hold the object of attraction in your right hand in front of the dog's head, just above eye level. Bring your right hand quickly down and out to a point in front of the dog as you say "down." Praise when he is down. You may give him the object briefly as a reward. Remember to take it from him with "give," and praise for his releasing the object. Repeat this exercise five times per session.

Sit from a Down with Object

The hand motion with your right hand is the same as for the Sit Sequence. Say "sit" as you make the motion. Keep your left hand in the collar at the back of the dog's neck to aid him into a sit, if necessary.

Stand—Sequence 2

Kneel next to your dog with him at your left side facing in the same direction you are. Place two fingers of your right hand in the collar under his chin, and give the verbal command "stand" as you pull him forward into a stand. This week, try not to touch him with your left hand in front of the stifles unless you have to. Practice this exercise for two minutes, keeping your dog standing still.

Turns in Place

Practice the Right-Turn in Place and the About-Turn in Place as you did last week, but use the following progression for the Sit. Transfer leash from your left hand to your right and grasp it close to the snap. Check straight up with your right hand and tuck your dog into a sit with the left. Say "sit" and praise. Practice each turn five times per session.

Right Turn

Assume Control Position and bring the rings of the collar to the back of your dog's neck. Position your right foot, say "Konrad, heel," and bring the left foot together with the right. Place your dog in a sit as described above. Praise, but do not pet.

About Turn

Assume Control Position, rings of the collar at the back of the dog's neck. Say "Konrad, heel," take two steps straight forward, turn in place

180° to the right, away from your dog, take two steps straight forward, and place your dog in a sit as above. Praise, but do not pet.

Automatic Sit in Motion—Sequence 1

With your leash over your shoulder, position the rings of the collar at the back of your dog's neck. Give your dog the command "Konrad, heel," walk forward four or five steps, then halt. As you stop, grasp the leash close to the snap with your right hand and, with your left hand, tuck your dog into a sit, saying "sit." Praise, but do not pet. Concentrate on keeping your body facing straight forward, and having your dog sit absolutely straight at your side. Practice five Automatic Sits before moving on to the next exercise.

Heeling Leash over Shoulder

Practice Heeling on Leash this week until you can walk for 15 paces in a straight line and make two about-turns with no tension on the leash. Remember to keep your hands off the leash.

Circles Right and Left

These circles are four feet in diameter, leash held in Control Position. For the Circle Left, keep your dog in heel position as you circle toward your left, walking *very slowly*. For the Circle Right, keep him in heel position as you circle to the right at a *trot*. Practice three circles each per training session.

Sit-Stay—Sequence 1

Bring the rings of the collar to the back of the dog's neck, between his ears. Fold your leash into your left hand so that it is taut, but not tight, over the dog's head. If possible, keep your left hand below your waist. Give the hand signal with your right hand, palm open, brought across your body directly in front of your dog's nose, saying "stay." Don't use your dog's name. Pivot directly in front of your dog, count, pivot back to heel position, pause, and release your dog.

Work on this exercise until your dog is staying in position up to a silent count of 30. When he has stayed to the count of 30 for 3 days in a row, further practice should be done with no tension on the leash.

Off-Leash Heeling—Sequence 1

Be sure to practice this exercise in a safe area. Position your leash for the slip release. Command "Konrad, heel," and begin to circle left. As you enter the circle, release your dog. Complete the circle and stop, sitting your dog by placing your right hand against his chest and tucking him into a sit with "sit." Praise. Do one off-leash circle to the left per session.

Long Sit—Sequence 1

Sitting in a chair, sit your dog at your side for 10 minutes three times this week. Your dog should remain in the sit position for the entire 10 minutes. At the end of that time, praise and release your dog.

Long Down—Sequence 2

Place your dog in the down position and sit in a chair. Your dog is to remain in the down position for 30 minutes. At the end of that time, release your dog and praise. Practice this three times this week.

Whistle Training—Sequence 1

Practice in a room with no distractions. Blow the whistle and reward your dog with a treat when he comes. Repeat until your dog is responding eagerly to the whistle, then practice three times per session.

6

Lesson 3

T HROUGHOUT THIS TEXT we refer to a
check on the leash. A check is a quick snap on the leash and an immediate
release, followed by praise. It is important for you to concentrate on the
release of tension on the collar after the snap. Under no circumstances
should you maintain an even tension on the collar, as that would teach your
dog to dislike training. Your checks should be quick and decisive, not slow
and nagging.

Your dog learns where his advantage lies through pleasant and unpleasant experiences. If your checks are ineffective and your praise is in-
sincere he will be unable to do so, and you in turn will not be successful in
your training.

Continue to refrain from petting your dog during training unless
specifically directed to do so. From now on, instructions will no longer include "do not pet your dog." It is understood that praise means verbal and
not physical praise.

If Konrad knows nothing else but to come when called, he would be an
acceptable pet. Next week we will teach you how to train your dog to come
when called. For this exercise he will have to know the Sit-Stay. So work
particularly diligently on Sit-Stays this week.

Last week you began teaching the dog an exercise called the
Automatic Sit. This is an important exercise and will determine the amount
of control you have over your dog. It is called the Automatic Sit because
ultimately the dog will sit at heel whenever you stop walking without any
further verbal command or physical assistance from you. He will learn to

do this in a series of progressions, leading up to his sitting automatically.

Heeling with Leash over Shoulder during Changes of Pace

Object: To accustom your dog to remaining at heel position when you go fast or slow.

Instructions: While heeling along with your leash over your shoulder, take two transition steps as you slow down into a very slow pace. Continue walking for ten paces slowly and then take two transition steps back into normal pace. To practice the fast pace, take two transition steps to gradually move into a trot. Trot for ten paces, and then take two transition steps back into normal pace.

Goal/Assignment: Work until you can change paces to walk slow and fast with no tension on the leash for ten paces each.

Watch for: On the slow pace, you will likely have to hold your dog back with your left hand on the leash to keep him in heel position. When you go back into normal pace, encourage your dog with a cheerful "Let's go" to remain in heel position.

When you go into the fast pace, encourage the dog to remain in heel position. If your dog becomes overly exuberant when you start to trot with him, check him back to heel position, and praise immediately as you remove your hand from the leash. The next time you go into a fast pace, don't go quite as fast so that you can keep your dog under control.

Whenever you change pace, do so gradually with two transition steps.

Sit-Stay—Sequence 2

Object: The next progression teaching your dog to remain in a sitting position on the command "stay" and not to move until released.

Instructions: Sit your dog at your left side and bring the rings of the collar under his muzzle. Fold the leash into your left hand, leaving about three feet of slack. Give the hand signal and command "stay," walk 3 feet in front of your dog, and turn and face him. Place your left hand, holding the leash, against your mid section so that there is only one inch of slack in the leash. Place your right hand, palm toward your dog, under the leash about half way between the two of you. At the first sign that your dog is thinking about moving, step toward him and slap the leash with your right hand. (The motion with your right hand is toward a point directly above your dog's head but not above your waist.) At the same time repeat "stay." Do not praise at this time. Remain in front of your dog for 10 seconds, then pivot back to his side, pause, praise, and release.

When standing in front of your dog, remain still and don't fidget to in-

Reinforcing the stay command.

Handler is prepared to reinforce the stay command.

sure you don't inadvertently cause him to move.

Goal/Assignment: Work up to a full-minute stay in front of your dog.

Watch for: It is during this exercise that you will learn to "read" your dog. Being able to read a dog means knowing what he is thinking and what he is going to do next. If you observe your dog closely, he will tell you. Is he thinking of staying or is his attention distracted by some leaves being blown across the yard, by some children playing down the road, or by a cat wandering by? If he turns his attention to anything other than you, he is not thinking about staying and you should immediately reinforce the command by slapping the leash to a point directly above your dog's head, at the same time repeating "stay."

You can also tell if your dog is thinking about coming toward you. His tail begins to wag and just before getting up, he will lean slightly forward. Intercept his thoughts before he has actually moved by following the procedure described above.

In case he has managed to move before you were able to reinforce the command, reposition him as quickly as possible at the exact spot where he had been left. Do so with a minimum of physical handling. Too much physical handling at this point may be construed by your dog as praise, obviously not the impression you want to create.

Remember that teaching your dog to stay is training for abstention—that is, not to move. When you reinforce the command by slapping the leash, do not follow this check by praise. The dog will be praised upon conclusion of the entire exercise.

Also remember that your dog learns by repetition. If you permit him to repeatedly break position, you are teaching him to break. Should this happen to you, go back to last week's assignment, making sure you and your dog are proficient before you go on.

Return to Dog on Stay

Object: To teach your dog to remain in position while you return to heel position by walking behind him.

Instructions: When you are standing in front of your dog, place the loop of the leash over your right thumb, and hold the leash loosely in your left hand, leaving about 3 feet of slack. Keep your left hand in front of your dog's nose throughout this exercise. Walk to your right by your dog's left side, then behind him, and then stop at his right side (your left) in heel position. Pause, praise, and release your dog.

Watch for: Do not apply any pressure against the dog's collar during this return. Your left hand should prevent the leash from pulling against the

Return to dog on the stay

Return around behind on stay.

Preparing for the sit

for

examination.

collar, or dragging across your dog's face or neck.

Be prepared throughout this exercise to check your dog back to his original position if he should try to move with you. If your dog is unsteady when you walk around behind him, practice sit-stays for a few days pivoting back to heel position, and then try the return again.

Sit for Examination

Object: Introduction to the Stand for Examination and the one exercise which endears obedience trained dogs to veterinarians and groomers.

Instructions: Sit your dog at your left side. Give the "stay" signal and command. Hold the leash folded in your left hand above your dog's head as you did in last week's lesson, remaining at his side. With the leash taut, have a friend or relative approach your dog from the front presenting the palm of his right hand to your dog. After your dog has had the opportunity to sniff the individual's hand, your assistant/friend is to run his hand lightly over your dog's head and back and then walk away. Your dog is to remain sitting throughout this procedure. If he attempts to move, check him straight up with your left hand and repeat "stay."

Goal/Assignment: Repeat this exercise until your dog remains steady in a Sit-Stay as he is approached and stroked.

Watch for: If you have a very excitable dog, be prepared to check straight up at the first sign of breaking. If you have a very shy dog, have the individual approach him with a treat. Whether or not your dog takes the treat is not important—it's the gesture that counts. The individual should also avoid eye contact with your dog as he offers the treat. A few positive repetitions like this and your dog will accept the examination, having forgotten about his apprehension.

Turns in Place: Right-Turn—Sequence 2

Object: The next progression of this exercise.

Instructions: Sit your dog at your left side and assume control position. This week, instead of placing your right foot prior to giving the command, give the command "Konrad, heel," and take a step to the right ¼ turn away. Sit your dog and praise.

About-Turn—Sequence 2

For the about-turn in place, take only one step forward, turn 180 degrees away from your dog, and take one step forward before sitting him. Praise.

Goal/Assignment: Do five of each turn per lesson.

Watch for: This week concentrate on getting quick responses from your dog. He should get up quickly when you say his name and "heel," and he should be sitting quickly after the turn.

Check your own posture carefully. Are you facing straight ahead and sitting your dog parallel to your left side?

Stand-Stay—Sequence 1

Object: To teach your dog to remain still in the standing position until released.

Instructions: Take the leash off and put it on the ground behind you and to your right. Stand your dog at your left side as before. Look to see that all four feet are comfortably underneath him. Stand erect next to your dog and give him the "stay" command and hand signal. Remain at your dog's side for 30 seconds, then praise him and release.

Goal/Assignment: Work up to a 3-minute Stand-Stay at your dog's side this week.

Watch for: Don't hover over your dog. Remain erect next to him and don't fidget. Motion from you might trigger the same response from your dog.

If your dog should move, place your right hand in the collar, your left hand against his stifles and reposition him, saying "stay."

Retrieving

Object: To utilize your dog's instinct to retrieve.

Instructions: Use a ball or other toy in which your dog is interested. Put the leash snap on the "dead" (non-choke) ring of the collar. Crouch down about five feet away from a wall. Tease your dog with the ball by showing it to him and immediately moving it away from his face. At the same time ask, "Want this? Look at this. Oh, boy! You want it?" Then roll the ball toward the wall saying, "Take it!" Praise when he picks it up. With a minimum of pressure, use your leash to guide your dog back to you, praising all the way. When he gets to you, say "give" and remove the ball from his mouth.

Goal/Assignment: Repeat three times per session.

Watch for: Be very careful not to check your dog during this exercise. It should be more like a game to your dog. If your dog is reluctant to go after the object, be sure that you are really teasing him excitedly. Try to work him into a very excited state before releasing the object with the command "Take it."

123

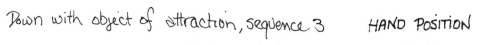
Down with object of attraction, sequence 3   HAND POSITION

Preparing for the down from front with object of attraction.

Down from front

with object of attraction.

If you cannot interest your dog in a ball, see if you can find something he will chase.

Some dogs are not interested in retrieving, and this is perfectly normal. If this is the case, don't make an issue out of this exercise right now.

Sit and Down—Sequence 3

Object: To teach your dog to respond to the commands and to enable you to position your dog from in front of him.

Instructions: With your dog sitting at your left side, tell him to "stay" and kneel directly in front of him. Fold the leash into your left hand, and place two fingers of your left hand in his collar under his muzzle. Hold the object of attraction in your right hand, in front of his eyes. Make the downward motion with your right hand as you say "down." Help your dog down by applying pressure downward on the collar with the left hand.

To sit your dog with the object of attraction, bring your left hand up to the back of your dog's neck. Make the motion with your right hand up over the dog's head, and if necessary, help your dog up by lifting with your left hand in the collar. As you motion with the object, say "sit." Praise.

Goal/Assignment: Repeat both the Sit and the Down with the object of attraction three times per session.

Watch for: Even if your dog goes down voluntarily, it is important that you apply downward pressure on the collar as this prepares him to go down with pressure alone, which is part of next week's lesson. This exercise conditions him to accept this pressure without resisting.

Long Sit—Sequence 2

Object: The next progression in teaching your dog to sit still.

Instructions: This week position yourself across the room from your dog as he sits still for 10 minutes. Remember, don't give a "stay" command.

Goal/Assignment: Repeat this three times this week for 10 minutes each.

Long Down—Sequence 3

Object: The next progression of this exercise.

Instructions: This week you will sit in a chair across the room from your dog for 30 minutes while he remains down. Do not move around the room. Remain seated for the entire 30 minutes.

Goal/Assignment: Repeat this three times this week, 30 minutes each. Practice the Long Down and the Long Sit on alternate days.

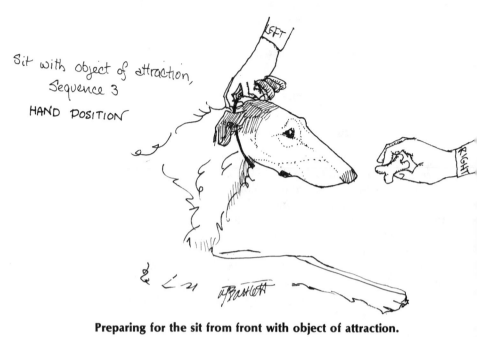

Sit with object of attraction,
Sequence 3

HAND POSITION

LFT

RIGHT

Preparing for the sit from front with object of attraction.

Retrieving Object

Put the leash snap on
the "dead" ring
of the collar...

Dead ring of the collar.

Whistle Training—Sequence 2

Object: The next progression of this exercise.

Instructions: Take your dog to a confined area outside such as a fenced yard, tennis court, Little League field, school yard or any similar place with no distractions. Let him off the leash and, when he is not paying any attention to you, blow the whistle. As soon as he comes to you, immediately reward with food and praise.

Goal/Assignment: Repeat three times per session. Try to take your dog to three different locations during the course of the week.

Watch for: If your dog becomes so interested in the treat that he won't leave your side after the first whistle blast, be satisfied with your success and go home. Try it again tomorrow.

LESSON CHECKLIST—Lesson 3

This week practice with your dog in different locations that are free from distractions. If you have been working in your back yard, work in the front. If you have a quiet park nearby, take him there to practice. Three times this week train your dog in a location unfamiliar to him, but as free from distractions as possible.

Heeling with Leash over Shoulder

Practice this week until you can walk for 20 paces, do an about turn, and walk for another 20 paces with absolutely no tension on the leash.

Circles

Continue to incorporate Circles Right and Circles Left into your heeling pattern. Remember to slow down and hold your dog back as you circle left and to move at a trot as you circle right. Practice three of each circle during each training session.

Change of Pace

As you are heeling along in a straight line or large counterclockwise circle, gradually change pace so that you are moving very slowly, walk for ten steps at a slow pace, then change pace gradually back to your normal pace. For the fast pace, change gradually to speed up to a trot, trot for 10 steps at the fast pace, then gradually slow down to your normal pace. Practice until you can move at the fast and slow paces for 10 steps with no tension on the leash.

Sit-Stay—Sequence 2

Bring the rings of the collar under the dog's muzzle. Give the "stay" command and signal, move 3 feet in front of your dog and turn and face him. Position your left hand holding the folded leash against your mid section with one inch of slack on the leash. Place your right hand, palm toward your dog, under the leash about midway between the two of you. At the first sign of your dog's thinking about moving, step toward him and slap the leash to a point directly above his head repeating "stay." Practice until you can remain in front of your dog for 1 minute without having to slap the leash to remind him to stay.

Return Around Behind on Stay

Place your right thumb through the loop of the leash and grasp the leash in your left hand, leaving about 3 feet of slack. Walk to your right— the dog's left—around behind your dog, and stop when you get back to his right side at heel position. Pause, praise, and release.

Sit for Examination

Have a friend or relative go over, offering the right hand to be sniffed, palm open toward the dog, and then lightly running the hand down the dog's back, and walking away. You should be at your dog's side holding the leash taut in your left hand over the dog's head. Tell him to "stay" before the person approaches.

Turns in Place—Sequence 2

For the Right-Turn in Place, say "Konrad, heel," then take a step to the right and sit your dog. Praise. Repeat five times per session.

For the About-Turn in Place, take one step forward, turn 180° away from your dog, take one step forward and sit your dog. Praise. Repeat five times per session.

Stand-Stay—Sequence 1

Take the leash off and put it on the ground behind you and to your right. This exercise is practiced off leash, so remember to take it off. Position your dog in a Stand, making sure that his feet are comfortably under him. Stand erect next to him, tell him to "Stay" as you give the hand signal, and remain at his side. Do not fidget. Begin at 30 seconds, and work up to a 3-minute Stand-Stay at your dog's side this week.

Retrieving

Put the leash snap on the dead ring. Kneel on the floor about 5 feet away from a wall. Get your dog very excited about the object you are using, and roll it toward the wall with the command "Take it." When he picks it up, praise, and guide him back to you with the leash, praising all the way. Tell him to "Give" and remove the object from his mouth. Praise. Repeat three times per session.

Sit and Down—Sequence 3

Kneel in front of your dog, holding the object of attraction in your right hand and having the leash folded into your left hand. Place two fingers of your left hand in the dog's collar under his neck. As you move the object downward and say "Down," apply downward pressure with your left hand in the collar. Repeat three times per session.

To sit your dog from the down with the object of attraction, bring your left hand to the top of the dog's neck, make the motion from in front of your dog's nose to above his head with your right hand as you say "Sit," and lift your dog with your left hand.

Down-Stay

Down your dog at your left side. Tell him to "Stay" as you give the hand signal. Walk 3 feet away and then turn and face him. Begin with a 1-minute stay before pivoting back to your dog, pausing, praising and releasing. Work up to a three-minute Down-Stay over the course of several sessions.

Automatic Sit

Review this exercise as you have been for the last week. Bring the rings of the collar to the top of the dog's neck and assume Control Position. As you stop, reach for the leash snap with your right hand. Check upward with your right hand as you tuck the dog into a sit with your left hand, saying "Sit." Praise as you hold him in position. Practice five Automatic Sits in motion during each session.

Off-Leash Heeling—Sequence 2

Be sure to practice this in a safe area. Position your leash for the slip release. Circle to the left with "Konrad, heel," and release. This week come out of the circle at a normal pace and continue for five steps before you come to a halt. As you stop, place your right hand against your dog's chest, and tuck him into a sit with the command "Sit." Praise. In case you are proceeding too quickly for your dog, never be afraid to go back to an earlier progression in which you achieved success.

Long Sit—Sequence 2

This week sit across the room from your dog as he sits still for 10 minutes. Practice three times this week.

Long Down—Sequence 3

This week you sit across the room from your dog as he does the Long Down for 30 minutes. Practice three times this week.

Whistle Training—Sequence 2

Practice in a confined area. Blow the whistle and reward/praise your dog for coming to you. Practice three times per session in three different locations.

7
Lesson 4

___

Now is a good time to examine how
your training program is progressing. We hope that you are enjoying the
developing relationship with your dog, and that your dog is also enjoying
his training.

It is important that you approach training with a positive attitude.
Your feelings will be reflected by your dog. If you are having fun, he'll have
fun. If you notice that when you pick up the leash your dog heads in the
other direction, this means that you have created a negative atmosphere.
Approach your training with enthusiasm and enjoyment and your dog will
respond in kind.

You have had a chance to observe your dog's reactions to specific
maneuvers. It is likely that on various occasions prior to the start of a new
exercise your dog has circled in front of you and you have guided him
behind your back to heel position. While this may have been easier, it is a
form of unintentional training. The dog is deciding how to line up and in
effect is training you. It is best not to permit your dog to circle you in this
fashion. Instead of permitting him to go around behind you, keep him at
your left side and line him up by taking several steps forward.

Moreover, whenever you want to line your dog up facing the opposite
direction, do so by making a small circle to the left. We know it seems a lot
simpler to turn to the right, away from your dog; however, you will have
much more success in your training by turning to the left, keeping your dog
at heel position and making him adjust to you, than by turning to the right.
This rule does not apply, of course, to Turns in Place or About-Turns

Encourage your dog as you start your turn

RIGHT TURN

Diagram for the right turn.

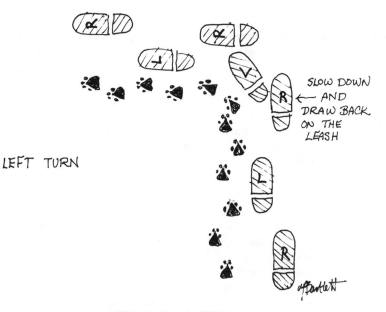

SPEED UP TO NORMAL

SLOW DOWN AND DRAW BACK ON THE LEASH

LEFT TURN

Diagram for the left turn.

while Heeling which are done to the right.

Heeling with Leash over Shoulder
Right- and About-Turns in Motion

Object: To teach your dog to remain in heel position when you make turns in motion.

Instructions: Select a tree, or position some objects, in your heeling area. If you heel along a street, practice this exercise at the corners. Make definite angle turns. For the Right Turn, encourage your dog to remain at your side as you turn to the right (making a 90° turn) and continue walking. For the Left Turn, slow down and draw back on the leash before you make the turn to keep your dog from getting ahead of you. Make the turn and resume your normal pace. Throughout both of these turns, your dog should remain in heel position.

Goal/Assignment: Practice five of each turn per training session.

Watch for: While you are turning, keep your feet close together so that your dog can remain at your left side.

Sit for Examination—Sequence 2

Object: The next progression of teaching your dog to allow friendly strangers to approach him.

Instructions: Leave your dog on a Sit-Stay and go 3 feet in front of him. Position your leash in your left hand, against your mid section, and have your right hand, palm toward the dog, under the leash. Be prepared to slap the leash and tell your dog to "Stay" at the first sign that he is going to get up. Have the stranger, a friend or relative, approach the dog from in front, offer his right hand, palm open, and then run the hand lightly over your dog's head and back.

Goal/Assignment: Repeat two or three times a session so that your dog becomes completely relaxed with this procedure.

Watch for: Be prepared to reinforce the "Stay" command at the slightest hint of breaking on the part of your dog.

Down Hand Signal—Sequence 1

Object: To teach your dog the hand signal for "Down" and another exercise to condition him to drop reliably.

Instructions: Leave your dog on a Sit-Stay and kneel on one knee in front of him. Fold the leash into your left hand and position two fingers of your left hand in the collar under his muzzle as you did for the Down Sequence 3 last week. The hand signal is given by raising your right hand and arm

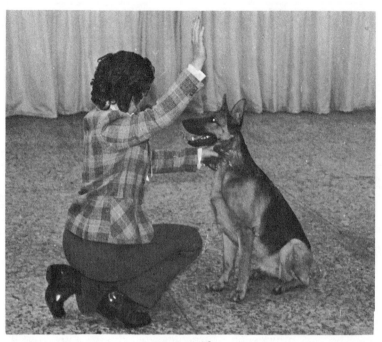

Down with

hand signal.

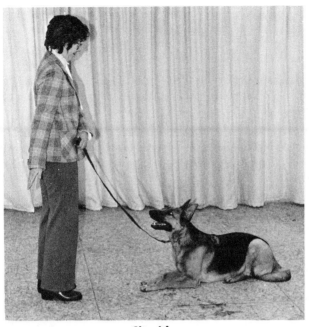

Sit with

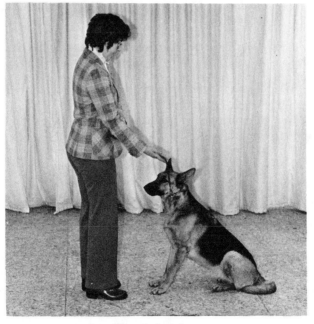

hand signal.

135

straight up. Command "Down," raise your right arm and, with your left hand in the collar, push back toward your dog's tail and then down. The backward pressure will push your dog slightly off balance so that he cannot resist the downward pressure.

Goal/Assignment: Repeat this exercise four times during each training session. This exercise is practiced together with the Sit Hand Signal which follows.

Watch for: Keep your back erect. Don't hover over your dog as you give this signal and command. Push back and down so that you will not get into a wrestling match with your dog. Be sure to keep the signal visible as you praise.

Sit Hand Signal—Sequence 1

Object: To teach your dog the hand signal for "Sit."

Instructions: Stand erect in front of your dog in the Down position. Fold the leash into your left hand so that it is taut between the two of you. Place your left hand against your right hip. The hand signal is given with the right hand, palm open and facing toward your dog. The motion begins at your right side, moves backward slightly, and then sweeps toward your dog in an upward motion toward a point directly over your dog's head, but not above your waist. As you sweep toward your dog, slap the leash as you say "Sit" and return your hand, palm open, to your side keeping it facing toward your dog as you praise.

Goal/Assignment: Repeat this four times during each training session in conjunction with the Down Hand Signal.

Watch for: If your dog is slow getting up, or reluctant to get up, make your slap of the leash a harder check.

Be sure to return your right hand to your side, palm facing toward your dog as you praise.

Stand-Stay—Sequence 2

Object: The next progression of this exercise.

Instructions: Stand your dog at your left side, get him comfortable, and give the signal/command "Stay." Step directly in front, remain there for 30 seconds, and then pivot back to heel position. Pause, praise, and release.

Goal/Assignment: Work up to 1 minute in front of your dog.

Watch for: If your dog is not steady for 30 seconds, do it for a shorter time, and gradually work up to 1 minute this week.

Hand position for
the automatic sit

Hand position for automatic sit.

Automatic   **sit.**

NOT THIS

A CHECK ACROSS THE OWNERS MIDLINE

RESULTS IN

A CROOKED SIT.

Incorrect check for automatic sit.

If you cannot move in front of your dog because he is still fidgeting, continue to work on last week's lesson.

Automatic Sit—Sequence 2

Object: The next progression of this exercise.

Instructions: Position the rings of the collar on top of the dog's neck. As you get ready to stop, grasp the leash close to the leash-snap with your left hand. The motion with your left hand will be to check straight up keeping your left forearm parallel with the dog's spine as you say "Sit."

Goal/Assignment: Repeat five times per session in motion.

Watch for: If your dog does not sit absolutely straight, or begins to sit crooked when you come to a halt, repeat "Heel," take another step forward, and physically place your dog in a straight sit as you have been for the past 2 weeks.

If your dog continues to try to sit crooked, examine your body posture and what you are doing with your left hand. If you check toward your body, or in a backward motion, this will cause your dog to sit crookedly or out of heel position.

Sit-Stay with Test

Object: To make sure your dog understands and responds to the "Stay" command.

Instructions: Put the leash on the dead ring and begin the exercise as you did last week. Signal and command "Stay," walk 3 feet in front of your dog, and turn and face him. Your left hand is at your midsection and the right hand is ready to reinforce the stay. With as little body or hand motion as possible, apply slight pressure on the collar toward you. This is accomplished by folding a few more inches of the leash into your left hand. By now you should be able to manipulate the leash with either hand so that you can do this without any unnecessary movements. If the dog begins to come to you, reinforce the command by slapping the leash with your right hand repeating "Stay." The first few times you try this, the pressure should be quite slight. As your dog becomes steadier, increase the pressure until, over the course of several sessions, your dog will visibly stiffen and resist every time you apply pressure.

Goal/Assignment: Physical resistance by your dog when you test.

Watch for: When you apply pressure be sure it is an even, gradual pressure and not an inadvertent check. This is not an endurance contest and the pressure should last only from 5 to 10 seconds before being re-

Correct position

for recall

with praise and petting.

140

leased. Be prepared to reinforce quickly, especially the first few times when your dog does not yet fully understand what is expected from him.

Recall—Sequence 1

Object: To teach your dog to come when called.

Instructions: Teach this exercise in a safe area because it is done off-leash from the beginning. If you cannot work in a safe area, put your dog on a long line to practice the recall.

Leave your dog on a Sit-Stay and walk about 15 feet away, less if your dog is unsteady that far away. Turn and face your dog. Count to five, kneel down, count to five again, place your hands, palms up, on top of your thighs. Smile, and in a very happy, pleasant voice call your dog by saying, "Konrad, come!" Continue smiling as he comes toward you and, when he arrives, PET and praise him for one full minute. Convince him that coming to you was his greatest experience of the day for him.

Goal/Assignment: Repeat three times per session.

Watch for: Make sure your dog does not come to you before you call him. If he is not steady on the stay, have someone else hold him until you call him. Don't shout "NO!" at him should he get up and start toward you before you have called him. If he does, say nothing. Simply reposition him at the exact spot where you left him, and this time have someone hold him until you call. It is definitely not a good idea to discourage your dog from coming to you, even if it is prematurely. Just make sure that the next repetition is a successful one.

Be sure you pause for a count of five before kneeling down and again for another count of five before calling your dog. Have your palms open on your lap rather than reaching out toward your dog. Reaching might cause him to stop before he gets to you.

Now that you are calling your dog from a Sit-Stay, it is important to continue working on the regular SIT-STAY in which you return to your dog before releasing him.

If your dog does not come when you call, try using a treat. If he still does not come, use a 15 foot long line (see the Equipment section in Chapter 3) and give him a check as you call him.

Different dogs will do different things at different times during this exercise. Some dogs will bolt or run the other way, in which case you use the long line for one week to prevent a second negative repetition. You must, however, vigorously check the dog at the point where he wants to take off, and then repeat the "Come" command, offering yourself as a "haven" after the check. You must repeat this procedure several times, each time checking with authority, until you see the desired response. All but the most recalcitrant bolter will perform correctly after about a week. Don't forget to praise lavishly when the dog gets to you, even if you had to use the long line. For the truly incorrigible bolter, you will have to use the compulsive recall described in Lesson 6.

Young dogs can be particularly trying in this regard. As a puppy, Konrad performed correctly—willing, eager and enthusiastic recalls. To all outward appearances he had mastered the exercise. Then one day he turns a deaf ear and runs the other way. What has gone wrong? Nothing, really. Konrad is going through the Flight Instinct Period described in Chapter 1. His instincts tell him to explore the great outdoors and ignore your "Come" command. The situation is easily remedied by putting Konrad on the Long Line for one week to prevent any further negative repetitions. As soon as he is over the Flight Instinct, he will once again do perfectly willing, eager, and enthusiastic Recalls.

Long Sit—Sequence 3

Object: The final progression of this exercise.

Instructions: This week you may move around the room while your dog sits still for 10 minutes. Do not do anything that will serve as a distraction to the dog, and do not do something, such as vacuuming, which will necessitate his moving out of your way.

Goal/Assignment: Repeat this three times this week, for 10 minutes each.

Long Down—Sequence 4

Object: The final progression of this exercise.

Instructions: This week you may move around the room while your dog remains Down for 30 minutes. As with the Long Sit, do not do anything that would require your dog to move out of your way.

Goal/Assignment: Repeat this three times this week, for 30 minutes each. Alternate days between the Long Sit and the Long Down.

Whistle Training—Sequence 3

Object: The final progression of this exercise.

Instructions: Continue practicing this exercise in a confined area. By now you will be able to tell whether or not your dog is reliably returning when you blow the whistle. Continue to give him treats every time he comes.

The value of this exercise is that it gives you a means of having your dog return to you from a distance if you take him for a walk in the country or a large open area. Only you can decide whether or not your dog is dependable enough to be trusted off leash under such circumstances.

This exercise is not a substitute for the Recall, and your dog should be trained to respond to both the whistle and the command.

Watch for: Don't overuse the whistle, or your dog will begin to ignore it.

Once your dog has been trained, it is not necessary to use food every time, but in order to retain the association between the whistle blast and the reward, food must be given frequently.

LESSON CHECKLIST—Lesson 4

Again this week, work in three new locations without distractions.

Heeling with Leash over Shoulder

Begin each day's session with a 2-minute heeling drill. Incorporate changes of pace—fast & slow—and Circles Right and Circles Left, three of each. If you have to check your dog, be sure to let go of the leash immediately. Heeling with your dog should be lots of fun for you and your dog. Be enthusiastic, be animated, and enjoy yourself, and your dog will respond in kind. Besides, it's good exercise!

Right and Left Turns in Motion

After your two-minute warm-up, practice going around trees or other objects in your training area or, when you come to a corner, making a Right Turn or a Left Turn. For the Right Turn, encourage your dog to stay next to your left leg. For the Left Turn, slow down and draw back on the leash with your left hand to keep your dog back as you turn to the left. Remember, these are square turns—90°. Practice three of each per training session.

Sit-Stay—Sequence 3

Practice as last week. Stand 3 feet in front of your dog, holding the leash against your mid section with your left hand, and keeping your right hand, palm toward your dog, under the leash ready to slap toward your dog. This week, work up to a two-minute Sit-Stay without having to slap the leash.

Sit-Stay with Test

Incorporate the test when you practice the Sit-Stay. Be sure you first put the leash on the dead ring of the collar. Apply an even pressure on the collar, gradually increasing the pressure until your dog physically resists. Test three times each session for 5 to 10 seconds each time. Be prepared to

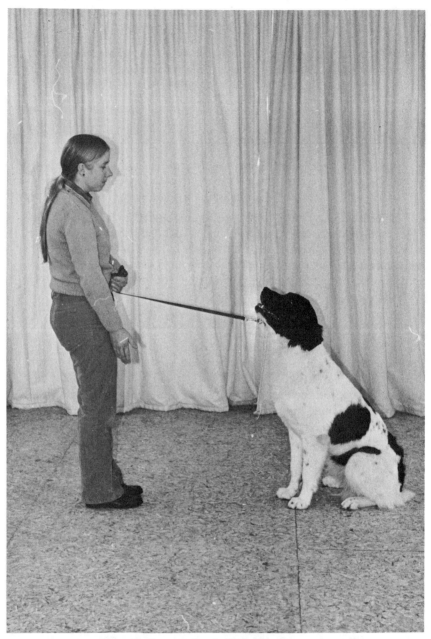

Sit-Stay on dead ring with test.

reinforce. Take this exercise seriously. There is no better way to condition your dog to the "Stay" command than this method.

Turns in Place

Work on this exercise as last week. Do four Right-Turns in Place and four About-Turns in Place during each practice session.

Sit for Examination—Sequence 2

This week you should be 3 feet in front of your dog as a friend or relative goes over your dog. Work on this over the course of several sessions until your dog is completely relaxed.

Sit and Down—Sequence 2 and 3

Review this exercise as last week. Do two Sits and Downs with the object of attraction while at your dog's side, and then move in front of him to do two of each from that position.

Down Hand Signal—Sequence 1

Kneel on one knee in front of your dog. Fold the leash into your left hand and place two fingers of your left hand in the collar under the dog's muzzle. Raise your right arm straight up. As you raise your arm, command "Down" and push back and down with your left hand. Keep your right arm in the signal position as you praise. Repeat four times per training session together with the Sit Signal.

Sit Hand Signal—Sequence 1

Stand erect in front of your dog. Fold the leash into your left hand, and place it against your right hip. Begin your hand signal with your right palm open at your side, fingers pointing down. Motion back slightly, and then forward toward your dog in a sweeping upward motion. Slap the leash upward as you bring your hand toward a point directly over your dog's head but not above your waist. Return your hand to your right side, palm open, as you praise your dog. Repeat four times per session.

Automatic Sit—Sequence 2

Bring the rings of the collar to the back of your dog's neck. As you prepare to stop, grasp the leash very close to the snap with your left hand. Keeping your left forearm parallel with the dog's spine, check straight up with your left hand as you say "Sit." Repeat five times per session.

Stand-Stay—Sequence 2

Stand your dog and leave him on a Stand-Stay. Step directly in front of him and remain standing still for 30 seconds, then pivot back to heel position. Pause, praise, and release. Work up to a two-minute Stand-Stay while you remain right in front of your dog.

Retrieving

Review this exercise as last week. Remember to put the snap of your leash on the dead ring before beginning this exercise. Practice three retrieves in a row. Remember, the command is "Take it!" Even if your dog really loves this exercise, do not overdo it. Always end this exercise with your dog wanting more.

Down-Stay—Sequence 2

Four times this week, do a three-minute Down-Stay with you 3 feet in front of your dog.

Off-Leash Heeling—Sequence 3

Review this exercise as last week. As you come out of the circle, continue for *10* steps before you stop. Make sure you pick up your pace as you come out of the circle.

Recall—Sequence 1

Leave your dog on a Sit-Stay, move about 15 feet away, turn and face your dog. Count to five before you kneel down. Count to five, place your hands on top of your thighs, palms up, smile, and call "Konrad, come!" Praise and pet him for one full minute. Practice three Recalls per training session.

Long Sit—Sequence 3

This week you may move around the room, but don't go out of sight. Repeat three times for 10 minutes each.

Long Down—Sequence 4

This week you may move around the room, but don't go out of sight. Repeat three times for 30 minutes each.

Whistle Training—Sequence 3

Continue to practice in a confined area. Don't overuse the whistle. Once your dog is trained, you don't have to reward with a treat every time, but it is best to do so frequently.

8
Lesson 5

THIS IS *Patience Week.* Some time between the 35th and 42nd day your dog, for several days, will give the appearance of having forgotten almost everything you have taught him so far. This phenomenon occurs with astonishing predictability and regularity. You will experience this with everything you teach your dog. Dog trainers refer to it as *plateaus.*

Don't become frustrated with your dog. We know you have just spent 4 weeks training him, and he has been doing ever so well. While it seems too much to bear, put up with him for the next few days and he will reward you by being better than ever before.

Continue to pay particular attention to the degree of precision with which your dog responds to you—it is in direct relation to the amount of control you have over your dog. While practicing, keep in mind that, contrary to popular belief, practice does not make perfect—only perfect practice makes perfect.

Heeling Hand Signal

Object: Introduction of the hand signal.

Instructions: With your dog sitting at heel position, the signal motion is given with your left hand, palm down, swept from left to right in front of your dog's face, as you say "Konrad, Heel."

Goal/Assignment: Repeat the hand signal and voice command when you begin heeling. It is not necessary to use the hand signal each time you begin heeling, but do repeat it at least five times per training session.

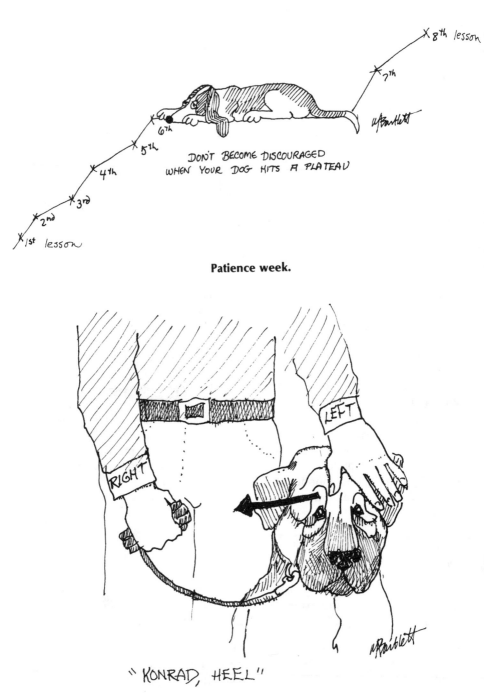

DON'T BECOME DISCOURAGED
WHEN YOUR DOG HITS A PLATEAU

8th lesson

7th

6th

5th

4th

3rd

2nd

1st lesson

Patience week.

" KONRAD, HEEL "

RIGHT

LEFT

Hand signal for heeling.

148

Sit-Stay—Sequence 4

Object: The next progression of this exercise.

Instructions: This week go out to the full length of your leash in front of your dog, 6 feet. Position your hands as you have been, left hand against your mid section, right hand poised under the leash ready to slap toward your dog at the first sign of his thinking about moving. Initially stay in front for 30 seconds. Return around behind, pause, praise, and release.

Goal/Assignment: Work up to a two-minute Sit-Stay over the course of several sessions.

Finish—Sequence 1

Object: This exercise teaches the dog to move to your side from in front of you with the command "Heel." It is one of the neatest exercises in obedience training and is a lot of fun to teach your dog.

Instructions: Leave your dog on a Sit-Stay and step directly in front of him so that your toes are not quite touching his. With the rings of the collar under the muzzle, fold the leash in your right hand. Place your left hand, palm down, on the leash-snap. Both hands are close together under the dog's muzzle. Command "Konrad, Heel," and, starting out on your right foot, walk straight ahead slightly to your right past your dog's left side to a point three or four steps beyond your dog. As you move past him, he will turn with you. As soon as both of you are again facing the same direction, tell him to "Sit" and place him if necessary. Praise.

Goal/Assignment: Five repetitions per training session.

Watch for: You will have to bend over if you have a small or medium-sized dog, but hold the leash short as instructed, no matter how much you have to bend. Rather than hovering over your dog, bend your knees.

As you are walking to your right, your dog's left, your dog should turn toward you so he is moving in a counterclockwise direction. Do not try to turn him away from you, to your left.

Remember, it is the dog that does the turning. You walk straight ahead. You don't turn.

Stand-Stay—Sequence 3

Object: The next progression of this exercise.

Instructions: This week, get your dog comfortably standing, give the signal/command "Stay" and go about 3 feet in front of him, then turn and face him. Remain there for 10 seconds, then return to heel position by pivoting back. Pause, praise, and release.

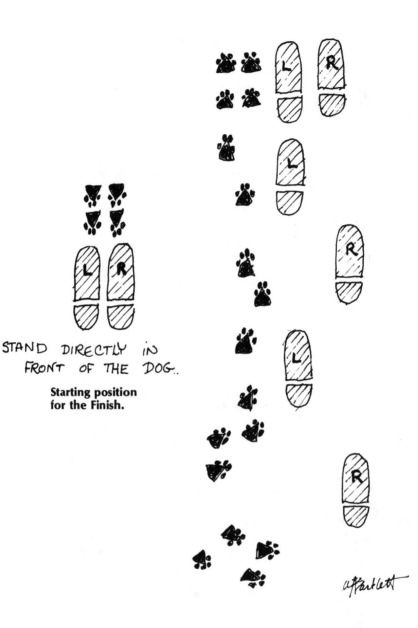

STAND DIRECTLY IN
FRONT OF THE DOG..

**Starting position
for the Finish.**

STEP OUT ON YOUR RIGHT FOOT
AND WALK STRAIGHT PAST THE DOG
FOR 3 OR 4 STEPS...

Diagram of the Finish.

150

Hand position for the Finish.

And

the

Finish.

151

Goal/Assignment: Over the course of several sessions, work up to a one-minute Stand-Stay with you 3 feet in front of your dog.

Watch for: If your dog should move, return quickly to his side, reposition him with a "Stay" command, and remain directly in front of him as you were last week. Work on this exercise closer to him until he is steady, and then go 3 feet in front again.

Stand for Examination

Object: To prepare your dog to be examined by someone other than yourself.

Instructions: Leave your dog as described above and pivot back after 10 seconds. Now examine your dog as though you were looking for something on his body. Go over him methodically but don't let him move. Start at the front end. When you are done, praise, pause, and release.

Goal/Assignment: Repeat once during each session.

Dumbbell Retrieve

Object: The next progression of the Retrieve exercise.

Instructions: Purchase a hardwood dumbbell of an appropriate size for your dog. They come in toy, small, medium, large and extra large sizes. Always hold the dumbbell by one of the ends, not the dowel. Attach the leash to the dead ring. Tease your dog with the dumbbell, talking in a very excited voice, and then toss it toward the wall with the command "Take it." When your dog picks up the dumbbell, praise, and bring him back to you. Command "Give," take the dumbbell, and praise. Repeat three times.

Goal/Assignment: Three repetitions per session.

Watch for: If your dog has absolutely no interest in the dumbbell, continue working with the object you've been using, and then try him again at another time. If he shows no interest in retrieving, don't make an issue of it now.

Down Hand Signal—Sequence 2

Object: The next progression of this exercise.

Instructions: Review last week's instructions and perform the exercise once with your dog before moving on to this progression. Then position yourself about 2 or 3 feet in front of your dog, on one knee. Give the hand signal and voice command "Down." If necessary, grasp the snap of the leash with your left hand and check your dog down. Praise.

Goal/Assignment: Four repetitions, in conjunction with the Sit Hand Signal.

Watch for: Do not pull the leash toward you. Be sure you check downward. You will have to reach toward your dog in order to do so. Leave the signal visible to the dog as you praise.

This exercise teaches your dog to go down in response to your hand signal. Once your dog has learned this, it is potentially life saving.

Caroline was walking her dog, Loki, off leash in a park when Leslie, her mother, approached from the other side of a busy street. Loki saw Leslie and immediately began to run toward her.

To stop Loki from crossing the street, Leslie raised her arm, giving the Down Hand Signal. Loki went down and waited for Leslie to cross the street to greet him. His response to the Down Hand Signal very likely prevented Loki from getting hit by a car.

Sit Hand Signal—Sequence 2

Object: The next progression of this exercise.

Instructions: Stand erect about 3 feet in front of your dog. Position the leash as last week, left hand against your right hip. As you give the hand signal with your right hand say "Sit," step toward your dog, and slap the leash upward.

Goal/Assignment: Four repetitions of each hand signal.

Watch for: Pause between repetitions of the Sit and Down Hand Signals. Don't teach your dog to pop up and down, but rather to wait for your signal/command. Count to 10 before giving the next signal.

It is not necessary for your dog to be looking directly at you in order for him to see your signal. Dogs have excellent peripheral vision. They can see very well to the side even if they are looking away. Therefore, don't engage in all manner of arm waving, foot stomping or saying "Psssst" to get your dog's attention prior to giving the signal. Give your signals as though your dog were looking directly at you.

In any case, even if he is not paying attention, and doesn't see your signal, you must convince him that it is his responsibility to be aware of what you are doing. You teach him this by giving the signal and then checking your dog if he fails to respond. If you wait to give your signal until he is paying attention, then he is training you.

Sit in Front—Sequence 1

Object: The first progression of teaching your dog to sit in front of you

Preparing

for the sit

in front.

when you call him.

Instructions: Take the leash off your dog and put it in your pocket. Stand your dog at your left side and command/signal "Stay." Step directly in front of your dog, toe to toe, and pause. Place two fingers of each hand, palms up, in the collar under the dog's neck on either side of his throat. Keep your back straight. Bend your knees if necessary, but do not hover over your dog. Command "Sit" and bring both hands up toward your waist, guiding him into a straight sit in front of you. Praise. Pivot back next to your dog to stand him and repeat the exercise.

Goal/Assignment: Repeat five times per session.

Watch for: Do not lift your dog's front feet off the ground. Do not push your dog backward into a sit. The dog will bring his rear forward into a sit if you simply hold the front end in position and keep his spine straight with equal pressure of both hands toward your waist.

If your dog tries to swing his rear end to one side or the other, this means that one of your hands is pulling more than the other.

Off-Leash Heeling—Sequence 4

Object: The next progression of this exercise.

Instructions: Once you and your dog have mastered last week's assignment, you can now try the slip release while heeling in a straight line or a large counter-clockwise circle. Put your dog on slip release and step out with "Konrad, Heel." After several steps, use a pay-attention check. A pay-attention check is just that—it reminds the dog to pay attention and concentrate. Then release your dog and continue for 20 steps or until you see the dog is about to make himself independent, whichever comes first. As you come to a halt, be prepared to help him into a sit by putting your right hand against his chest and tucking with your left.

Goal/Assignment: Twenty steps off-leash heeling with your dog remaining in heel position.

Watch for: It is important that you maintain an even pace before, during, and after the release. Walk briskly so that your dog must keep his attention on you. Under no circumstances should you slow down after the release because this will confuse your dog. Be sure that you don't change your body posture after the release. Above all, don't turn the upper part of your body to look back at your dog as that will cause him to fall behind you; this is called lagging. Keep him in sight by looking down at him. If you can't see his head, then he is somewhere other than in heel position.

Be satisfied with 20 steps of good off-leash heeling. If you push the dog and he makes a mistake, you are teaching him to make that mistake. Since there is virtually nothing you can do by way of remedial action when the dog is off leash, it is best to end your practice of off-leash heeling after each successful repetition. This way your dog is conditioned in a positive manner to perform the exercise correctly.

Recall—Sequence 2

Object: The next progression of this exercise.

Instructions: Leave your dog on a Sit-Stay, walk 15 feet away and turn to face him as you did last week. This week count to 10 before kneeling. Again, count to 10 before calling "Konrad, Come." Smile. Remember to have your hands on top of your thighs, palms up. When he arrives in front of you, as you are telling him what a marvelous dog he is, reach over and tuck him into a sit in front of you. Do this without using a "Sit" command. Hold him in position for a count of 10 and then praise and pet him for one minute.

Goal/Assignment: Do three recalls per session.

Watch for: For the dog who is slow to respond and the one who sometimes comes and sometimes does not, a treat provides the incentive to come more quickly and more reliably. Show your dog the treat and put it in your pocket. Continue with the exercise as instructed and give your dog the treat when he gets to you. Don't wave the treat at your dog as that would become an additional signal, a form of unintentional training.

For two weeks, give him a treat every time he comes. After two weeks, reward him at random. If the recall becomes slow again, reward more frequently.

LESSON CHECKLIST—Lesson 5

Part of your assignment this week is to make several excursions to a park or a shopping center parking lot to work your dog. This will condition your dog to respond under all circumstances. He has reached the point that he should be able to pay attention even if there are other people and noises around.

Heeling Leash over Shoulder

Begin each training session with the 2-minute heeling drill. Include Circles Right (2), Circles Left (2), changes of pace to fast and slow, remembering to change pace gradually.

Hand Signal for Heeling

The hand signal is with your left hand, palm open and facing down, brought from left to right in front of your dog's eyes as you give the command "Heel." Incorporate this hand signal into your heeling.

Sit-Stay and Sit-Stay with Test

This week you are 6 feet away from your dog. Work up to a two-minute Sit-Stay. Remember to return around behind. Test your dog with pressure on the collar after you have put it on the dead ring. Test twice during each session.

Finish—Sequence 1

After completing the Sit-Stay, heel your dog to a different area in which to work on this exercise. Leave your dog on a Sit-Stay and step directly in front of him, toe to toe. Fold the leash into your right hand, and place your left hand near the snap of the leash, palm down, under the dog's muzzle. Keep your hands close together. Give your dog the command "Konrad, Heel," and walk straight ahead to your right, three or four steps past your dog, and place him into a sit at heel position. Repeat five times per session.

Right and Left Turns

As a separate exercise from your two-minute heeling drill, practice making Right, Left and About-Turns in motion. Keep your dog at your left side throughout the turns, and keep your feet together as you are making the turns. Practice three of each turn per training session.

Stand-Stay—Sequence 2

Leave your dog on a Stand-Stay and go 3 feet in front, and turn and face him. Remain there without fidgeting and pivot back to heel position. Work up to a one-minute STAND-STAY 3 feet away.

Stand for Examination

Leave your dog and after 10 seconds, pivot back. Methodically examine him, starting at the front and working your way to the rear. After you are done, praise, pause, and release.

Dumbbell Retrieve

Transfer the snap of the leash to the dead ring. Tease your dog and get him very excited about the dumbbell and toss it toward the wall with the command "Take it." Praise when he picks it up, and bring him back to you.

Have him "Give" and praise. Remember, always hold the dumbbell by the end. Repeat this no more than three to five times per session.

Down-Stay—Sequence 3

This week stand 6 feet in front of your dog. Begin with a one-minute Down-Stay, and work up to a three-minute Down-Stay. When you return, go around behind your dog as you have been doing with the Sit-Stay.

Turns in Place

Practice the Right-Turn in Place and the About Turn in Place three times each session.

Down Hand Signal—Sequence 2

Begin each practice session with one review of last week's work, then perform this exercise from 3 feet in front of your dog. Kneel on one knee, give the command and hand signal. If necessary, grasp the snap of the leash with your left hand and check downward. Leave your arm erect as you praise. Pause for a count of 10 before sitting your dog.

Sit Hand Signal—Sequence 2

Stand erect 3 feet in front of your dog. Position the leash in your left hand, which is placed against your right hip. Give the signal with your right hand, palm toward your dog, then step toward your dog and slap the leash as you say "Sit." Return your hand to your side, palm open, as you praise. Pause for a count of 10 before downing your dog. Do four repetitions of each of these hand signals.

Automatic Sit

Position the rings of the collar at the back of the dog's neck. As you come to a halt, grasp the leash close to the snap and check straight upward as you say "Sit." Remember to keep your arm parallel with your dog's spine and to make your check straight up. Repeat five times per session.

Sit in Front—Sequence 1

Stand your dog with his leash off and step directly in front. Place two fingers of each hand in the collar under the dog's neck, and keep your back straight. Say "Sit" and guide the dog into a straight sit in front of you. Pivot back to heel position and stand him again. Repeat five times per session.

Off-Leash Heeling—Sequence 4

This week release your dog as you are heeling in a straight line or in a large counter-clockwise circle. Do not change your pace before, during, or after your slip release. After your dog is off leash, continue heeling for 20 paces, then stop and sit your dog. Give a pay-attention check before you release.

Recall—Sequence 2

After you have left your dog, pause for a count of 10 before kneeling and pause for a count of 10 before calling him, palms up on thighs. The command is "Konrad, Come." Smile and receive him with loads of praise. As you are praising him, reach over and tuck him into a sit in front of you without a command and continue praising for one minute. Repeat three times each session.

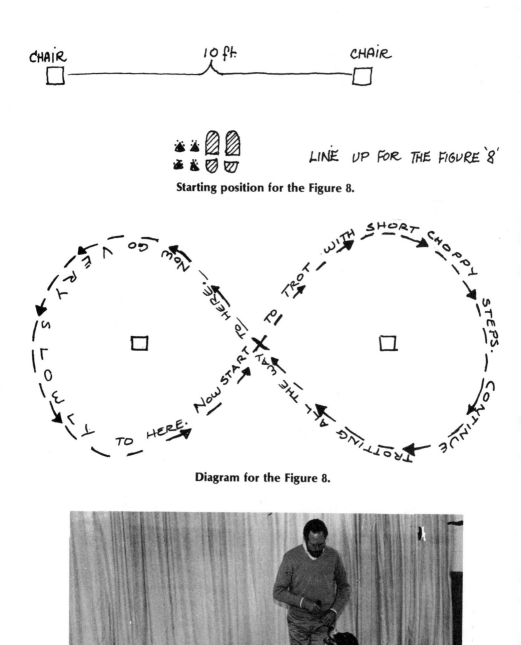

Starting position for the Figure 8.

Diagram for the Figure 8.

The Figure 8.

9

Lesson 6

WEEKS 5 AND 6 are *Patience Weeks*. See opening page of Chapter 8.

Figure 8

Object: To accustom your dog to remain at your side and not to interfere with you as you move in different directions.

Instructions: Position two chairs or other objects about 10 feet apart. Place yourself with your dog sitting at heel position 2 feet from the center line between the two objects. Assume control position, and keep your hands in front of your legs at all times throughout this exercise. Command "Konrad, Heel," and begin by trotting around the post to your right and then going slowly around the post to your left, making a Figure 8. Circle each post three times and then stop and sit your dog.

Goal/Assignment: Make three trips around each post during each training session.

Watch for: Your change of pace into the Fast should begin just before you cross the imaginary "X" in the center of the 8 so that you are moving at a nice trot as you make your circle to the right. Continue trotting until you have again crossed the "X" and are beginning to circle to the left. At that point, slow way down.

Do not let your left hand fall behind your left leg. Keep both hands firmly planted against your thighs in front of your legs. When you trot, make short choppy steps so that your dog can stay with you without fishtailing. Halt at different locations instead of always stopping at the same point.

Return

on

the

stand.

Stand-Stay—Sequence 4

Instructions: Go out 6 feet in front of your dog and turn and face him. The first time you do it wait for 10 seconds before returning to him.

Goal/Assignment: Increase the time you remain in front to 1 minute over the course of several sessions.

Stand for Examination—Sequence 2

Object: The next progression in teaching your dog to be examined by someone other than yourself.

Instructions: With the leash off, stand your dog, signal/command "Stay" and step directly in front of him. Have a family member or friend examine your dog. Have the person approach the dog from in front, offer his right hand palm open and then run the hand lightly over your dog's head and back.

Goal/Assignment: Repeat one time per training session.

Watch for: Be prepared to verbally reinforce the stay command at the slightest hint of breaking on the part of the dog. He may move his head but not his feet.

Return to Dog on Stand

Instructions: From now on, when you return to your dog walk around behind him as you have been for the Sit-Stay and Down-Stay. The first few times you try it, steady him by placing two fingers of your left hand on his withers as you walk around behind his tail and back to heel position. You can eliminate placing the two fingers on his withers as soon as he stands perfectly still while you return.

Retrieving

Object: To introduce your dog to objects of different materials.

Instructions: In addition to continuing to work with the dumbbell, this week introduce your dog to retrieving other objects, such as metal cans. Six-ounce juice cans work well with most dogs.

Goal/Assignment: Three retrieves per session.

Watch for: Don't allow your dog to chew the can. Have him bring it directly back to you.

Voice Command Down

Object: To teach your dog to respond to the verbal command "Down" without any motion or signal.

Instructions: Sit your dog at your left side. Fold the entire leash into your left hand. Place two fingers of your left hand in the collar, palm facing down. Say "Down" and if your dog does not respond, apply downward pressure on the collar.

Goal/Assignment: Repeat two times per session.

Watch for: Do not get into a contest of strength. If your dog does not readily respond to the command and pressure with your left hand, continue work with the object of attraction for another week, and then try this exercise.

Finish—Sequence 2

Object: The next progression of this exercise.

Instructions: Review Sequence 1 twice, then leave your dog on a Sit-Stay, step directly in front and hold the leash as you did before. With "Konrad, Heel," take two steps backward guiding your dog around to your left in a counter-clockwise circle, and then take two steps forward. Command "Sit," and praise.

Goal/Assignment: Two of Sequence 1 and five of Sequence 2 each session.

Watch for: Be sure you are taking two steps backward and two steps forward. If you have a very large dog, you may need to take three or four steps backward and three or four steps forward.

Do not drag your dog around. If he seems reluctant to perform this progression of the exercise, practice Sequence 1 for several more days to accustom him to getting up and moving on the command "Konrad, Heel."

Each session, review the previous progression twice before practicing the new sequence.

Sit in Front—Sequence 2

Object: The next progression of this exercise.

Instructions: Take the leash off and put it in your pocket. Leave your dog on a Sit-Stay, go about 3 feet in front and turn and face him. Call him with the command "Konrad, Come." When he is directly in front of you, reach down to place two fingers of each hand in his collar and guide him into a sit in front with the command "Sit" as you did last week. Praise. Count to five, tell him to stay, back up and repeat. After five repetitions, tell him to stay, return around behind him to heel position, pause, praise, and release.

165

The second

progression

of the Finish.

166

THIS...

NOT THIS

Correct and incorrect body posture and position of hands for the front.

Goal/Assignment: Five per session.

Watch for: Wait until your dog is directly in front of you before reaching down to grasp his collar. If you reach out toward him as he is coming in to you, it will cause him to stop, and some dogs will actually bolt.

   If he does not move at all on the command, put his leash on to get him started coming toward you. Once he is moving, proceed as above.

Recall—Sequence 3

Object: The next progression of this exercise.

Instructions: Leave your dog, count to 10, crouch down with your hands on your thighs, count to 10 and call your dog. As he approaches, stand erect so that you are standing up when he gets to you. When he is directly in front of you, grasp the collar as above and sit him with the command "Sit." Praise. Count to five, tell him to stay, and walk around behind him to heel position.

Goal/Assignment: Three recalls per session.

Watch for: As for the Sit in Front, don't reach out toward your dog. Wait until he gets to you before you reach down to guide him into the Sit in Front.

   If at any time during your work on Recalls, your dog doesn't respond to your command or takes off in another direction, put him on a Long Line for further practice for several weeks. Do not permit a repetition of this negative experience. By keeping him on a Long Line you will teach him to come when called and prevent his running away from becoming a habit.

   Once he has taken off in another direction, to get him to come to you, there are several maneuvers which are effective in most instances.

   Rather than run after your dog, which he interprets as a game with you joining him, run away from him screaming like a banshee. The effect this has on most dogs is one of intense interest in the seemingly irrational behavior on your part. It also reverses the game, causing him to chase you.

   Once your dog is more interested in you than in running away, stop and catch him with lavish praise.

   Another maneuver to get your dog to return to you is to sit or lie down on the ground and intently carry on a conversation with the grass. Talk in an intimate yet animated manner. Few dogs will be able to resist investigating the object of your interest. The trick here is to appear completely disinterested in what your dog is doing until you have a firm hold on him. Then praise.

   Once you have had to go through one of these maneuvers you should not do any more training for several hours. Under no circumstances should

168

you punish your dog once he has come to you.

These tricks work a few times. They will not work with the chronic runaway and are not a substitute for training.

Compulsive Recall

For the chronic runaway, you may wish to consider the Compulsive Recall, which is done as follows: put your dog on a Sit-Stay, and go to the end of the leash. Call him with "Konrad, Come," and at the same time vigorously check toward you. Repeat this five times, each time checking just as firmly as the first time even though he now appears to come willingly.

To be effective, your checks must be such that there is absolutely no doubt in his mind that it is much more advantageous to come when called than to run the other way. Praise lavishly when he gets to you and give him a treat. Convince him that coming to you is the greatest experience of his day. Repeat this procedure for five sessions before trying him off-leash again. If he still bolts, start all over, this time checking even more firmly since you did not get the desired response up to now. You may have to go to a pinch collar.

A dog does not turn into a chronic runaway overnight. This is a learned response which, through many repetitions, has become a habit. To break this habit will require many repetitions of the Compulsive Recall.

It is critical during this training period that you interrupt the behavior pattern by preventing further recurrences. This is accomplished by keeping the dog on leash or a long line so that he cannot run away any more.

If, despite all your precautions, your dog manages to get away from you, do not chase him. And once he comes back, or you catch him, never punish him. He will only associate the punishment with getting caught, not with having run away or not coming when called. You must try to praise him sincerely, even if you are livid when he comes back to you.

LESSON CHECKLIST—Lesson 6

This week concentrate on practicing on different surfaces. If you have been training primarily on grass, work on pavement, or vice versa.

Also this week, firm up the Sit-Stay and Down-Stay on different surfaces such as linoleum, carpet, grass, pavement and stone.

Continue to take your dog to shopping centers and parks to work him around mild distractions. Make three more excursions this week.

Heeling with Leash over Shoulder

Begin each day's session with a two-minute heeling drill. Time yourself to make sure you are in fact heeling for 2 minutes. Incorporate Circles, Changes of Pace and the Heeling Hand Signal. Try the Heeling Hand Signal without any voice command. Continue to use the voice command with and without the hand signal.

Sit-Stay with Test

Review your Sit-Stay With Test once, leash on the dead ring, before doing a Sit-Stay at the end of the leash.

Sit-Stay—Sequence 5

From 6 feet in front of your dog, increase the amount of time you are away from him. Aim for a three-minute Sit-Stay. Take your dog to different areas on different surfaces for one-minute stays from 6 feet away. This is less involved than it sounds when you consider that in your home you probably have at least three different surfaces—concrete, linoleum or tile, and carpet. You can readily incorporate practicing Sit-Stays on these surfaces into your daily routine with a minimum of effort on your part.

Figure 8

Place yourself with your dog at heel position 2 feet from the center line between two posts placed 10 feet apart. Keeping your hands in front of your thighs at all times, heel around the two posts, going slowly around the left one and moving at a trot around the right one. Circle each post three times.

Stand-Stay—Sequence 3

Remove your leash and go 6 feet in front of your dog. Work up to a one-minute Stand-Stay. Return around behind your dog at the end of the exercise, pause, praise, and release.

Stand for Examination—Sequence 2

Remove the leash, stand your dog, and step directly in front of him. Have a helper go over your dog. Return to heel position, pause, praise, and release. Repeat once per session.

Retrieving

Accustom your dog to retrieving metal articles. Use a can of appropriate size for your dog, and make a game with it as for all other retrieving. Continue to work on the dumbbell retrieve as well. Practice three retrieves per session with the metal article and three with the dumbbell.

Right-, Left- and About-Turns

Continue to work on your turns in motion—Right, Left and About.

170

Remember to keep your body facing straight ahead and your feet close together as you execute the turns. Do three of each turn during each training session.

Voice Command Down

Sit your dog at your left side and fold the leash into your left hand. Place two fingers of your left hand in the collar, palm down. Command "Down" and, if he fails to go down on the command only, apply downward pressure with your left hand in the collar. Praise. Repeat this three times before doing a Down-Stay.

Down-Stay—Sequence 4

Give the command "Down" without any body motion. When he is down, command "Stay" and go 6 feet in front. Work on this exercise on different surfaces for one-minute Down-Stays. As always, return around behind, pause, praise, and release.

Automatic Sit—Sequence 3

Continue to practice this as you did for the past few weeks. Do five Automatic Sits per training session. If your dog *begins* to sit crooked, tell him to "Heel," take several steps forward, and make him sit straight. Avoid negative repetitions.

Off-Leash Heeling—Sequence 5

Continue to practice this exercise. It may be necessary for you to do a brief Heeling With Leash Over Shoulder exercise before doing the slip release for Off-Leash Heeling. As you come to a halt, tell your dog to "Sit" and have him come to an Automatic Sit off leash.

Give your dog a pay-attention check before the release so your dog's attention is on you when you slip the leash. Watch your pace so that you don't slow down after you have slipped the leash.

Finish—Sequence 2

Review Sequence 1 by repeating it twice before each day's practice on this progression. Stand in front of your sitting dog, hold the leash short in both hands, keep your hands close together, command "Konrad, Heel," take two steps backward as you turn your dog toward you in a counterclockwise direction, then take two steps forward while guiding him into heel position with "Sit." Praise. Repeat five times per session.

Down Hand Signal—Sequence 3

From 3 feet in front, stand erect as you give the command and signal with your right hand. Review two times with signal and voice and then try the signal alone without voice command. If your dog fails to respond, keep your hand up, step toward your dog, and check straight down with your left hand. Praise. Do not pull the leash toward you. Count to 10 before sitting your dog. Repeat four times per session in conjunction with the Sit signal.

Sit Hand Signal—Sequence 3

Stand erect as you give the command and signal with your right hand. Be sure to slap the leash as your right hand comes up and toward your dog. Review two times with signal and voice command and then try the signal alone without the voice command. Be sure that you slap the leash even though you are not saying anything to your dog. Count to 10 before downing your dog. Repeat four times per session.

Turns in Place

Review three Right-Turns and three About-Turns in place during each training session. Concentrate on getting perfectly straight sits each time you turn.

Sit in Front—Sequence 2

Stand 3 feet in front of your sitting dog. Call him with the command "Konrad, Come." As he arrives in front of you, reach down to place two fingers of each hand in his collar, and guide him into a sit in front. Praise. Count to five, tell him to STAY, back up and do it again. When you have done five repetitions, tell him to stay, return around behind, pause, praise, and release.

Recall—Sequence 3

Count to 10 before crouching down, count to 10 before calling your dog and, as he is heading in toward you, stand erect. When he arrives in front of you, reach down as for the Sit in Front and guide him into a straight sit in front of you. Praise. Tell him to stay, walk around him to heel position, pause, praise, and release.

10

Lesson 7

Automatic Sit

Up to now you have been practicing the Automatic Sit by checking straight up with your left hand as you halt and at the same time saying "Sit." The purpose of the previous progressions has been to provide your dog with a firm foundation for this important exercise. As stated in Lesson 3, your goal is to have your dog sit at heel when you come to a halt on his own, without any further verbal command or physical guidance from you.

With the foundation he has now received, you are ready to eliminate the first of the two inducements you have been using—the verbal command "Sit." From now on, when you come to a halt and when you practice Automatic Sits, check straight up, but eliminate the "Sit" command.

Stand Hand Signal

Object: To introduce the hand signal for the Stand.

Instructions: Sit your dog at your left side. Place two fingers of your right hand in the collar under the dog's muzzle. The hand signal is given with your left hand, palm down, in a motion from right to left in front of the dog's eyes and parallel to the ground. As you give the signal and command, take one step forward on your right leg and close with your left. Keep your body facing straight ahead.

Goal/Assignment: Five times per session.

Watch for: Be sure that your body is facing straight ahead and that you don't turn toward your dog. Your dog should come to a stand in heel position. You should both be facing in the same direction.

If your dog wants to sit after you have taken one step forward, try it

Hand signal

for the

stand.

Assisting the dog into the stand.

174

again—only this time continue moving your left hand around to the dog's right hind leg to assist him in standing after you have given the Stand Signal.

Left-Turn in Place

Object: To teach your dog to make a Left-Turn in Place.

Instructions: Assume Control Position. Place your left foot directly in front of your dog's with your left foot facing to the left at a 90° angle. With, "Konrad, Heel," take a large step with your right foot beyond the left and close with the left. Sit your dog. Praise.

Goal/Assignment: Repeat five times per session.

Watch for: Be sure your angle is 90° and not 180°. This is a quarter-turn to the left. It teaches the dog to adjust himself to heel position and aids in the ultimate control you have over your dog.

Be sure your right foot steps beyond your left so that your dog will have room to get up and move to the left.

Place your left foot in front of your dog's feet prior to making the turn.

Finish—Sequence 3

Object: The next progression of this exercise.

Instructions: Review Sequence 1 twice and Sequence 2 twice. Then leave your dog on a Sit-Stay, step directly in front and hold the leash as you did before. Stretch your left foot way out to your left side and behind you at about a 45° angle. Command "Konrad, Heel" and guide your dog in a wide circle around to heel position as you bring your left foot even with your right. Keep your right foot glued to the ground.

Goal/Assignment: Practice three per session after reviewing Sequences 1 and 2 twice each.

Watch for: Your left foot must be stretched way back and out to the side in order to enable your dog to make a semi circle at your side and come back to heel position. If your foot is too close to your body, your dog can't go far enough away from you and will not have room to turn.

If your dog resists this maneuver, continue work on Sequence 2 for several days, and then try again.

Recall Hand Signal

Object: To introduce the hand signal for the Recall to your dog.

175

LEFT TURN IN PLACE

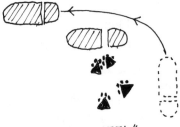

KONRAD, HEEL"

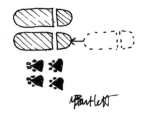

Diagram for the Left-Turn in Place.

Left-Turn

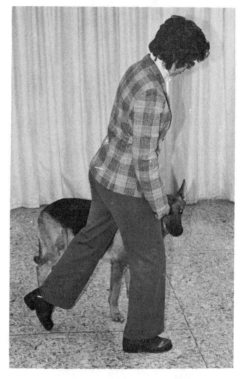

in

Place.

177

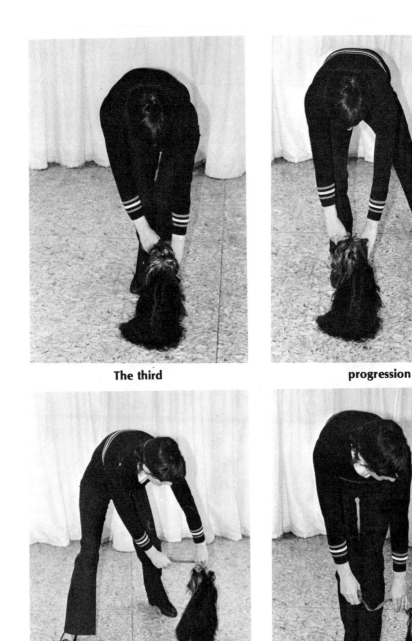

The third　　　　　　　　　　**progression**

for the　　　　　　　　　　**Finish.**

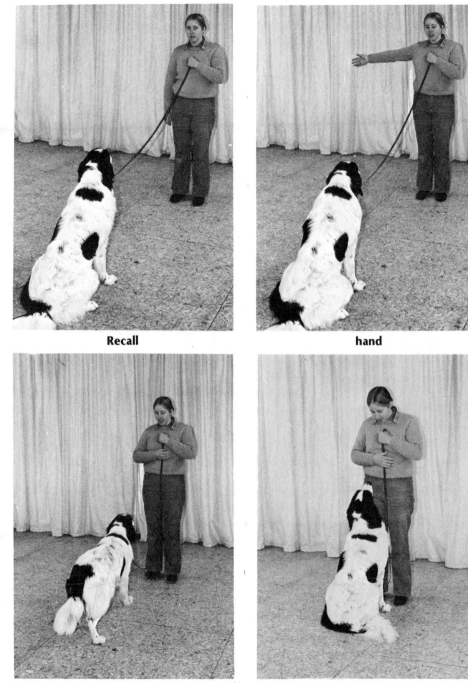

Recall

hand

signal

with Sit in Front.

Instructions: Leave your dog on a Sit-Stay and go 6 feet in front of him. Hold the leash in your left hand, and place your left hand against your chest so that the leash is taut. The hand signal is given with the right hand, brought up in an arc from your right side to shoulder height and then in a sweeping motion toward your chest. As you bring your hand to your chest, slap the leash with "Konrad, Come." Sit him in front with "Sit." Give him a verbal "Stay" command, back up, and try it again.

Goal/Assignment: Five repetitions per session.

Watch for: Be sure that your signal is away from your side rather than in front of your body. Your dog will not be able to see the motion from a distance if it is right in front of your body.

LESSON CHECKLIST—Lesson 7

Heeling with Leash over Shoulder

Begin each day's session with a 2-minute heeling drill. Incorporate Circles, Changes of Pace, and the Hand Signal for Heeling. Occasionally use the Heeling Hand Signal only without any voice command, and sometimes use the voice command without any hand signal. Mix it up.

By now you should be noticing a rhythm developing between you and your dog as you heel. This is achieved by maintaining a brisk pace throughout your two-minute heeling drill. Moving at too slow a pace provides too many opportunities for your dog to look around and become distracted or not to pay attention to you. Remember, the best pace for heeling is a hurried walk.

Sit-Stay with Test

Review Sit-Stay with Test, leash on the dead ring. Your dog should now be perfectly comfortable with this exercise, and you should be able to apply enough pressure to get physical resistance on the part of your dog for 15 seconds. Your dog should be visibly resisting your pressure.

See how hard you can pull with steady pressure before his rear end comes off the ground. This will give you an idea of his understanding of the word "Stay." When you have pulled hard enough to get this result, immediately release your pressure. If at any time he does not resist with his full weight, you should immediately check him back into position.

Sit-Stay—Sequence 6

Practice a one-minute Sit-Stay 6 feet away from your dog, then return around behind, pause, drop your leash at his side, repeat "Stay" and go 6 feet in front of him for a count of 10. Return around behind, pause, praise

Heeling with Leash over Shoulder.

and release. Work up to a one-minute Sit-Stay with the leash dropped next to your dog.

Figure 8

Continue to work on this exercise around two posts approximately 10 feet apart. Remember to keep your hands in front of your thighs at all times. Go slowly around the left post and trot around the right post. Make three trips around each post during each training session.

Stand Hand Signal

Place two fingers of your right hand in the collar under the dog's muzzle. The hand signal is given with your left hand, palm open and parallel to the ground, moving from right to left in front of your dog's eyes. As you give the signal/command, take one full step forward on your right leg, and close with your left. Keep your body facing straight ahead so your dog is standing at heel. Practice five times per session.

Stand for Examination—Sequence 3

This week go 3 feet in front of your dog, facing him as your helper approaches, offers his hand to be sniffed, and touches your dog on his head and back. Repeat once per session.

To steady your dog for this exercise, follow the procedure outlined below.

Stand-Stay Review

Each day practice the previous day's procedures, in order, one time. Then practice the new procedure five times. If you encounter any difficulty on any day, do not proceed to the next day's exercise until you have successfully accomplished what you are working on. Remove the leash before beginning this exercise.

Praise with your voice. Keep your hands off your dog as much as possible in this exercise. Keep your dog in a standing position as you praise. Release with much enthusiasm.

This is an ideal exercise to practice before you feed your dog— separate and apart from his outside training session.

Day 1   Stand your dog. Remain at his side. Keep your dog standing perfectly still for 2 minutes. Pause, praise and release.

Day 2   Review Day 1, then stand your dog, command "Stay," pivot in front, count to 10 and pivot back to your dog. Pause, praise and release.

Day 3   Review Days 1 & 2, then stand your dog, command "Stay," pivot in front, count to 20, pivot back to your dog, pause, praise and release.

Day 4   Review Days 1, 2 & 3, then stand your dog, command "Stay," go 3 feet in front of your dog and face him. Count to 30, then step back to his side. Pause, praise and release.

Day 5   Review Days 1, 2, 3 & 4, then stand your dog and command "Stay." Go 6 feet in front of your dog, turn and face him. Count to 30 and return around behind your dog to heel position, pause, praise and release.

Day 6   Review Days 1, 2, 3, 4 and 5, then stand your dog and command "Stay." Go 6 feet in front of your dog and face him. Count to 60 and return around behind your dog to heel position. Pause, praise and release.

Retrieving

Continue working with your dumbbell and other articles. This is a fun exercise for your dog and one that enables you to maintain his enthusiasm for his training.

Left-Turn in Place

Place your left foot in front of your dog's feet at a 90° angle. With "Konrad, Heel" take a large step with your right foot and close with your left. Repeat five times per session.

Finish—Sequence 3

Review Sequences 1 and 2 twice each. Then place your left foot way out to the side and behind you. Say, "Konrad, Heel," and guide your dog into heel position as you bring your left foot even with your right. Sit him at heel. Praise. Repeat three times per session.

Down Hand Signal—Sequence 4

Stand 6 feet in front of your dog when you give the hand signal and voice command "Down." If your dog does not respond immediately, step toward him and check him down with your *left* hand, keeping your right hand raised. Repeat four times per session, pausing for 10 seconds before sitting your dog in conjunction with the Sit Signal.

Sit Hand Signal—Sequence 4

Stand 6 feet in front of your dog when you give the hand signal and voice command. Slap the leash as you bring your hand upward toward your dog. Repeat four times per session. Do two with the voice command, then try two without the voice command and without slapping the leash. If your dog fails to respond to the command without the slap, repeat three times, with a check upward each time, and then try again with the signal alone.

Turns in Place

Review three Right-Turns and three About-Turns in Place during each training session.

Down and Down-Stay—Sequence 5

Down your dog by the voice command only. If your dog does not go down on the first command, reinforce with pressure on the collar. Leave him on a stay and stand in front of him for one minute, then return to him. Now drop your leash, tell him to "Stay," and go 6 feet in front again. Remain in front for 2 minutes before returning to heel position, pause, praise and release.

Automatic Sit—Sequence 4

This week, during each practice session do three Automatic Sits— each time checking the dog upward, as you have been for the past several weeks, with the command "Sit." Then do two Automatic Sits, checking upward without the "Sit" command.

Off-Leash Heeling—Sequence 6

Continue to work on this exercise, and this week incorporate one about-turn per session. Just before you make the turn, call your dog's name to make sure his attention is on you. If at any time your dog leaves heel position when you slip the leash, be sure to use the Slip Surprise for at least the next three times you slip the leash.

When using the Slip Surprise, check your dog at the precise location he previously left your side, and remember, you must check him three times, whether or not he attempts to leave your side again.

Sit in Front

Review this exercise from 3 feet in front of your dog. Pause before you give the command "Konrad, Come." Remember, don't reach out toward your dog. Wait until he is directly in front of you before grasping his collar to guide him into a straight sit in front. Praise. Repeat four times.

Recall Hand Signal—Sequence 1

From 6 feet in front of your dog, place your left hand, holding the loop of the leash, against your chest. Make the hand signal with your right hand brought up from your right side in an arc and sweeping across in front of you to slap the leash as you say, "Konrad, Come." Have him sit straight in front with "Sit." Praise. Repeat four times.

Recall Sequence 4

Leave your dog on a Sit-Stay, go 15 feet away, turn, count to 10, and remain erect as you call "Konrad, Come." Don't forget to smile. When he gets directly in front of you, help him into a straight sit. Count to five, tell him to stay, and return to heel. Practice three recalls per training session.

It is beneficial to continue training your dog in new areas away from home—a location unfamiliar to your dog without distractions.

11

Lesson 8

YOUR ATTITUDE toward training will reflect itself in your dog's attitude. If you are enthusiastic, your dog will be enthusiastic; if you are consistent and train him regularly, your dog will be reliable; if you are precise, your dog will be precise.

Automatic Sit Progressions

At this point you can expect that your dog has a good understanding of the Automatic Sit. When you come to a halt, he now sits quickly and straight at heel without the need for any further command or check from you. If he does not, this is a good week to review the Automatic Sit by practicing the progressions that you used to teach this exercise to your dog.

Sequence 1: Place your right hand on your dog's chest. Begin with your left hand at the withers. Say "sit," as you stroke down the dog's back with your left hand, over the tail and tuck him into a sit by applying pressure behind the stifles. Praise. Concentrate on keeping your body facing straight ahead and lining your dog up next to your thigh.

Sequence 2: Bring the rings of the collar to the top of the dog's neck. As you begin to come to a halt, grasp the leash snap with your right hand. Check upward with your right hand as you tuck your dog into a sit with your left, saying "sit." Praise. Again, make certain that you are not turning your body toward your dog, but are lining your dog up at your left side, facing straight ahead next to you as you are facing straight ahead.

Sequence 3: Bring the rings of the collar to the top of the dog's neck. As you prepare to stop, grasp the leash close to the snap with your left hand. Keeping your left forearm parallel with the dog's spine, check straight up with your left hand as you say "sit." Praise. If he begins to sit crooked, say "Heel" and take a step forward. Position him as for Sequence 2.

Sequence 4:   Three Automatic Sits, check as for Sequence 3, and say "sit." Then do two Automatic Sits, checking upward with your left hand, but without saying "sit."

Sequence 5:   For the first three Automatic Sits, check straight up as you come to a halt but do not say "sit." Then try two without checking.

Your dog's performance determines the particular progression you will have to review and emphasize. If he is sitting, but not sitting straight, you should go back to Sequence 2 so that you can control where your dog sits. Be sure that when you come to a halt you face straight ahead. Do not turn your body toward your dog, as this changes heel position. Keep your body straight, bend at the knees not at the torso, and check straight up with your right hand. Upon completion of the check, your right hand should be at a point directly above the dog's head, and not somewhere in the vicinity of your belt buckle.

If your dog is sitting straight but not quickly, you should review progression 3 or 4. When you check, be sure you do so with authority, and again, be careful that you don't draw your hand across your body.

Sit-Stay—Sequence 7

Instructions: At this point in your training, begin increasing the distance you stand in front of your dog. Whenever you begin to increase distance, initially decrease the length of time you are away from him. For example, you have been standing in front for 3 minutes at 6 feet away. When you drop the leash and stand 10 feet in front, do so for only 10 seconds the first time you do it. You can then rapidly increase the length of time until you are standing in front at a 10-foot distance for one minute.

Goal/Assignment: This week, work up to a one-minute Sit-Stay at a distance of 20 feet.

Watch for: If at any time your dog seems apprehensive having you that far away, decrease your distance and work on stays closer to your dog for a few days. Then when you increase your distance again, do it for a very short period of time before returning to your dog. Don't forget to pause, praise and release.

If you cannot get 10 feet away from your dog without his getting up, go back to previous progressions of the Sit-Stay and work until your dog is staying in place without moving. Test several times to reinforce in his mind what you want.

Figure 8

Instructions: Make three trips around each post—going slowly around the left post and trotting around the right one—then stop and sit your dog. Then make one full trip at a normal pace. Your dog should continue to change his pace—he will need to slow down as you go around the left post and speed up as you walk around the right post—but your pace should remain constant and brisk.

Watch for: Maintain an even pace as you go around each post. On the left post think slow and on the right post think fast. If your dog gets ahead of you on the inside turn or falls behind on the outside turn, continue to practice as before for several more days, and then try the normal pace again.

Finish—Sequence 4

Instructions: Review Sequences 1, 2 and 3 twice each. Then stand in front of your dog as for the previous progressions, holding the leash with both hands close together and close to the collar. With "Konrad, Heel" move your left leg out to the side and behind, and then bring it even with your right again, simultaneously guiding your dog into heel position. If necessary, check your dog into a straight sit.

Goal/Assignment: Review Sequences 1, 2 and 3 twice each, then practice three of Sequence 4 for three sessions.

Watch for: Note that this progression differs from Sequence 3 in which you first placed your left leg and then guided your dog to heel. In Sequence 4 you are guiding the dog and moving your left leg at the same time.

When your dog gets to heel position, you can now expect him to sit automatically without a "sit" command. If he does not, check straight up as for the Automatic Sit. Do not, however, repeat the "sit" command even if you have to check. The object of this exercise, as explained in Lesson 5, is for the dog to respond to the command on his own. This means that when he is fully trained to do this exercise, he will move on command from the Sit in Front to a Sit at Heel without any physical help from you.

If your dog doesn't have room to turn, let out a little more leash and move your entire upper body as you guide him around to heel position. If he resists this step of the exercise, continue working on Sequence 3 for a few more days and then try it again.

Finish—Sequence 5

Instructions: Review Sequences 1, 2, 3 and 4 twice each. Then stand in front of your dog and command "Konrad, Heel." By now you can expect him to go to heel position without any further physical guidance on your part. If he does not, firmly check in the same direction you have been guiding him for Sequence 4, but keep your feet stationary.

Goal/Assignment: Review Sequences 1, 2, 3 and 4 twice, then practice three of Sequence 5 per session.

Watch for: If your dog resists the finish, or seems confused, return for several days to a previous progression with which he is comfortable before going to the next sequence.

If your dog is anticipating your verbal command by beginning to move as soon as you move in front of him or as soon as you place your hands under his muzzle, prevent him from moving, and get him used to your standing in that position for 10 seconds before you tell him to "Heel." Insist that he wait for your command rather than going to heel position on his own.

LESSON CHECKLIST—Lesson 8

Heeling on Leash

Continue to practice your two-minute heeling drill as a warm-up each day. Include Circles and Changes of Pace. Occasionally use the Heeling Hand Signal without a voice command, and continue to use the voice command with no hand signal as well.

Sit-Stay—Sequence 7

Begin increasing your distance but remember to decrease your time as you do so. Begin 10 feet away for 10 seconds. Work up to 1 minute at that distance, then move to 15 feet for 10 seconds. When you can stay at that distance for 1 minute, move to 20 feet for 10 seconds and work up to a one-minute stay at 20 feet. Occasionally test your dog.

Down-Stay

Work on this exercise as for the Sit-Stay. You should be able to progress quickly on this exercise since your dog is used to staying down for long periods of time. Increase the amount of time you are in front of your dog to 3 minutes at a 20-foot distance. Remember, do so gradually as for the Sit-Stay.

Figure 8

This week, after you have made three trips around each post, going slowly around the left post and trotting around the right, stop and sit your dog. Then do one complete trip at a normal pace.

Stand Hand Signal

Continue to practice this hand signal with the voice command. Remember to move your left hand straight out from your side in front of your dog's eyes as you take one complete step forward and keep your body facing straight ahead to stand your dog. Do three repetitions of the hand signal, and then work on a Stand-Stay.

Stand-Stay

Do a one-minute Stand-Stay each training session. Have a helper examine the dog three times each week with you 6 feet away.

Retrieving

Continue to work with the dumbbell and other articles as you have been. Work on at least three retrieves per training session. If your dog is reliably bringing the object back to you, you may now take him off leash for this exercise.

Finish—Sequence 4

Review Sequences 1, 2 and 3 twice each. Then leave your dog on a Sit-Stay, step directly in front and say, "Konrad, Heel," moving your left foot out to the side and behind as you guide him into heel position. Praise. Repeat three times per session. Practice this sequence for 3 days.

Finish—Sequence 5

Review Sequences 1, 2, 3 and 4 twice each. Then stand in front of your dog and command "Konrad, Heel." If he does not move to heel position by himself, firmly check in the same direction you have been guiding him in Sequence 4. Keep your feet stationary. Repeat three times per session.

Sit and Down Signals

Continue to work on this exercise as you have been. Do three repetitions of each hand signal, no voice command. Remember to pause for a count of 10 between sits and downs.

It is important that you continue to count to 10 between the Down and Sit signals. If you do not separate these two commands with a short period of time, your dog will begin to anticipate the sit from the down and complete it on his own without waiting for your command or signal. This is called *anticipation* and is not desirable. The object of training is that the dog respond to your commands and not to a memorized sequence.

190

Turns in Place

Do three repetitions of the Right-Turn and the About-Turn in Place during each training session.

Left-Turn in Place

Place your left foot in front of your dog's feet at a 90° angle. With "Konrad, Heel" take a small step with your right and close with your left. Repeat five times per session.

Automatic Sit—Sequence 5

Do five Automatic Sits per training session. Review whichever progression is necessary in order to get your dog to sit automatically without any voice command or check. Sequence 5: For the first three Automatic Sits, check straight up as you come to a halt, but do not say "sit." Then try two without checking.

Off-Leash Heeling

Continue to perfect this exercise. Incorporate an About-Turn in Motion, a Right-Turn and a Left-Turn. Call your dog's name as you turn. If he is not right with you, go back on leash and check him at the exact point where he needs to be reminded to remain in heel position.

Sit in Front

Continue to work on this exercise as you have been. Practice four Sits in Front per training session. You can do this in conjunction with your practice of the Recall Hand Signal.

The ultimate object of this exercise is for the dog to come when called and sit directly in front of you without a "sit" command or physical guidance from you. At this point in your training your dog should be sitting on command only without any additional physical guidance. By the same token, you should not permit him to sit crooked. If he begins to sit crooked, immediately guide him into a straight sit by taking two steps backward. Keep in mind that every repetition, correct or not, constitutes training to the dog.

Recall Hand Signal

Stand erect facing your dog. Always pause before you give the signal/command. Remember to slap the leash as you call your dog. When he gets to you, tell him to "sit" and guide him into a straight sit. Tell him to "stay," back up and do it again. Repeat four times per session.

Recall

Work on this as you have been. Remain erect when you call your dog and, when he arrives, tell him "Sit." If necessary, guide him into a straight sit in front. Count to 10, tell him to stay, and return to heel position. Repeat three times per session.

Because it takes the dog from 35 to 42 days to learn a specific exercise, you will have to continue training your dog for 3 weeks beyond the completion of these lessons. For instance, the learning of the Recall, which was introduced in Lesson 4, will not be complete until the 10th week of training. The learning of the Finish, which was introduced in Lesson 5, will not be complete until the 11th week of training, or 3 weeks from now.

Even when you consider your dog fully trained, you should continue to practice with him on a regular basis. Your dog's response to commands gives him a job to do. This makes him feel important, which is so necessary for his continued mental health.

If you should run into any problem or regression in connection with these obedience exercises, review the progressions with your dog. Remember that after the passage of time the association between commands and responses will weaken. Your dog will need periodic refreshers to strengthen the associations. Do not believe that, just because he knew a command at one time, he will know it forever without periodic reminders. You yourself have probably forgotten many things you once knew well. Yelling at him will not make him remember—only a refresher training session will strengthen the association.

As we said before you began this training program, the dog is never wrong. If you live by this philosophy, you will always treat your dog fairly. You will have a mutually satisfying and rewarding relationship for many years.

192

12

Behavior Problems

As MENTIONED EARLIER, there are two purposes to dog training: the first is to teach your dog *to do* something, or to respond to your command, and the second is to teach your dog to refrain from doing something. In the process of teaching your dog to do something he will often stop doing many things that you find objectionable. For instance, if Konrad is being a pain in the neck, you can spend the better part of the day telling him all the things he *shouldn't* do: "Get out of the garbage! Don't go in there—I just washed the floor! Get off the couch! Don't bark! Don't jump on me—I'm dressed for work! Get off the counter! Drop that Kleenex!" On the other hand, you can use the positive approach. You can say, "Konrad, COME! Good boy! DOWN. Wow! What a good fellow!" And both you and Konrad feel better. He's not acting up any more, so you can relax, and he has been rewarded for doing a job for you.

It may not seem like much to you, but to dogs, working for their people by responding to requests and commands, no matter how simple, and getting praise for their efforts makes the whole day worthwhile. Sure, dogs love to play and chase sticks and get petted and cooed at, but when you get right down to it, all that is frosting. For the dog, the real cake is to have a function—a job to do.

It is through training that your dog learns to function as a contributing member of the household. Therefore, all of our cures for behavioral ills are based on the assumption that you are presently teaching, or have already taught, your dog to respond to commands, and that you use these commands frequently, regularly and with praise.

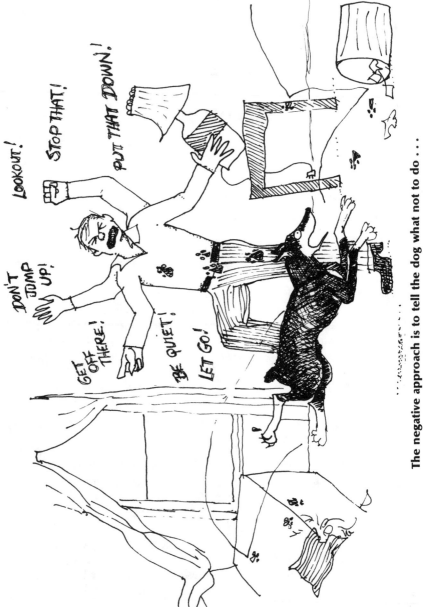

The negative approach is to tell the dog what not to do....

but the positive approach is more relaxing for both you and the dog.

195

Each behavior problem will be examined from the following points of view: Why is your dog doing this? What does he get out of it? Why don't you want him to do it? Does he understand that it is wrong? Can it be prevented? How can you change his behavior?

Why Does He Do it, or What's in it for Him?

Remember, dogs have no knowledge or understanding of human morality. They are amoral. Their behavior is unrelated to any human values involving a sense of duty or fair play. Every behavior your dog exhibits involves some sort of reward for him. For instance, taking food out of the garbage is rewarding to a dog.

Dogs don't do things for spite, to get even, or to teach you a lesson. Your dog is not chewing the couch every day because he's mad at you for leaving him alone while you are at work. He's not punishing you for anything you did or did not do. Dogs do not hold in their negative feelings. Tension-releasing behavior involves a reward system comparable to our blowing off steam.

Dogs don't get ulcers from worry, or heart attacks from tension. When they feel angry, frustrated or tense, they act out their feelings immediately and in clearly recognizable form. When you begin examining your dog's behavior, keep in mind that he is trying to tell you something is wrong.

It is important to understand the rewards involved in each behavior. In most cases, eliminating the reward is enough to eliminate the problem behavior. In others, some remedial training may be required.

Why Don't You Want Him to Do It?

What may be a behavior problem to some is perfectly acceptable behavior to others. A dog owner with a Yorkshire Terrier may not consider it objectionable if Little Tyke sits on his lap during dinner. For the owner of a Mastiff or Newfoundland, this would be most objectionable. Many dog owners don't mind their dogs jumping on them, but others do.

In the context of behavior problems you must first examine what it is you find objectionable and whether or not your objections are reasonable. You must keep in mind that Konrad is a dog, and be realistic in your wishes. If you can't stand hair on the floor, then a German Shepherd Dog or an Alaskan Malamute is the wrong breed for you. To have a dog who sheds and then to be angry with him because of it is unrealistic.

If you don't want to allow your dog to be a dog, you shouldn't have one. We once knew a woman whose dog would put his nose against the windows in her car when he rode with her. This behavior annoyed her. She wanted to keep a muzzle on him to prevent it. We suggested she ride with a bottle of Windex or leave the dog at home, or confine him in a crate in the car so he couldn't reach the windows. In others words, allow the dog to be a dog and ignore a few smudges.

Sometimes you may object to a certain behavior at some times and not at others. For instance, it may be okay for Konrad to jump on you when you're in grubby jeans, but not when you're dressed up. Or it's okay as long as his feet are clean, but not when it's raining and his feet are muddy.

This kind of inconsistency is enough to drive a sane dog crazy. How is Konrad to know which ones are your designer jeans and which are for cleaning the house? You must make up your mind that either you don't object to the behavior, or you do. Not sometimes, but all the time.

Does He Understand That It Is Wrong?

Konrad knows that lying on the couch is comfortable. He learned that as a young puppy when you allowed him there. This comfort, no matter how brief, is his reward every time he gets on the couch. In addition, Konrad has learned through repetition that every time you now enter the living room and he is on the couch, you yell at him.

Konrad, being no dumb animal, learns that when he hears you coming, he can quickly get off the couch and you don't yell at him. "Aha!" you say. "Konrad *knows* it is wrong to be on the couch. Why else would he get off when he knows I'm about to catch him on it? Anyway, he looks guilty!"

Let's examine this. Your yelling at Konrad for being on the couch does not alter the fact that the couch is comfortable to lie on. That remains true no matter how many times you yell at him. All Konrad learns from your yelling is that he'd just as soon you stayed out of the living room and left him in peace on the couch. So *lying on the couch* does not become a bad thing to do just because you yell. What is bad is that *you come into the room.*

And the guilty look? Remember, it's apprehension and fear. Konrad has learned that when you come into the living room and find him on the couch, he gets yelled at. He never will learn from this that *getting on* the couch is objectionable, only that *being on the couch when you are present* is.

In some cases, your dog may make the association between his action and your displeasure, and he may be aware that you object to his behavior, but the rewards may be stronger than your displeasure. We will go into specific instances where this may be applicable under each problem area.

Can Problem Behavior Be Prevented?

Problems can be avoided by using a little common sense and thinking ahead. For instance, you know you left the chicken carcass from last night's dinner in the garbage. You can take the garbage out before you leave the house, or you can leave it and take a chance on Konrad's polishing off the carcass. A little prior planning and some common sense can prevent a great deal of trouble for both you and your dog. Putting the garbage in the cupboard, or out of reach will save you lots of frustration.

It is especially important to think ahead when training puppies. Get into the habit of imagining how he will behave when he is an adult. It may be cute for a puppy, but will you want him to do it when he is grown? This is one example where an ounce of prevention is worth a pound, and many weeks, of cure.

How to Modify Konrad's Behavior
Using a Positive Approach or "The Cure"

There are as many different approaches to solving behavior problems as there are experts who think them up. We're sure that many of you have tried "everything," including the suggestions of such dog experts as your local gas station attendant. When it comes to curing behavioral ills, everyone is a doctor.

We believe that, for curing most problems, it is more fair to Konrad (and far more pleasant for both of you) to use a positive approach. Our cures may involve some modification of both your behavior with your dog and the situation that is causing the problem. In some cases it will involve changing the environment to a certain extent, but this approach neither blames poor Konrad, nor punishes him for behavior he honestly didn't know was wrong.

Some of the advice for solving problems refers to specific training techniques which are covered in the lessons. To solve such a problem, you will first have to train the dog.

Your dog's behavior problems did not occur overnight, and the solutions to these problems are not magical. Just because you have begun to train your dog and to give him a function does not mean that he will suddenly stop acting up. Some problems will disappear more quickly than others. Some will take several weeks, or even months, before you will be satisfied with your dog's behavior. Often, part of the solution to a behavior problem will involve a change in diet or spaying or neutering. Before undertaking the behavior modification programs outlined in this chapter, reread the sections, "What Does Konrad Eat?" and "Spaying and Neutering" in Chapter 2, You and Your Dog.

If you are not willing to spend the necessary time and energy required to solve your dog's problems, perhaps you should consider putting him up for adoption. On the other hand, if you are interested in your dog and believe, as we do, that a few weeks training and problem solving is little enough time to give your dog in return for the many years of pleasure and devotion he will give you, the following problem-solving techniques will help you achieve a harmonious relationship.

198

Begging

Begging food from the dinner table is one of the easiest things to teach a dog, and one of the hardest habits to break. Konrad's training to beg begins when he is a young, adorable puppy. "Oh, he's such a cute thing. This little piece of fat won't hurt just this once." It does not take too many repetitions before Konrad learns that he gets fed from the table by begging. Then Konrad sits by your chair while you are eating and stares at you. Occasionally he'll get up on his hind legs and paw you, or he'll nudge your arm and remind you that he is waiting. And he drools—that's the worst part. He looks as though you never feed him. Of course you give him a little tidbit each time. Who can resist those pleading eyes?

If you don't have this problem, prevention is quite simple. Don't start giving your dog food from the table—*ever*. If you must give your dog table scraps, give them in moderation and in his own dish after you have finished eating or, better yet, with his regular meal.

Once you have a dog that begs, it becomes a self-perpetuating problem. Begging is rewarded with food.

Chances are, if you have this problem you've tried to stop his begging—you've yelled at Konrad when he begs, pushed him away, and even gotten really angry, but he just gets more persistent. So you've had to give him *something* just to be able to eat in peace. What you have done is to reward his persistence. Each time you have tried holding out longer, but have ultimately given in, you have further trained him that no matter how far away the rainbow looks, there is a pot of gold at the end if he simply waits.

Some people don't mind their dog begging when they are alone, but it's embarrassing when they have company. Remember, you can't have it both ways. Konrad will either beg at the table, or he won't—not sometimes, but all the time.

When you are tired of this behavior and want to end it, when you get to the point that you can't stand the drooling, the whining, the pawing and the sad eyes staring at you, then you have to steel yourself for the cure.

Using the positive approach, give Konrad the command "DOWN"— place him down if necessary—and have him do a LONG DOWN by your chair during dinner. Be prepared for many interruptions initially, while you reinforce Konrad's DOWN. Each time he gets up, you re-command and re-place if necessary so that he remains down during your dinner.

With a truly recalcitrant begger, one that you have systematically trained to be persistent, your first week of dinners may be quite a trial. Some dogs bark repeatedly and go through all manner of random actions to try to get you to feed them from the table. But once you have begun this rehabilitation program, stick with it. If you give in at any time, no matter how small the tidbit you sneak him, not only have you lost that battle, you

Don't give in to those pleading eyes.

may very well have lost the entire war. If you have made up your mind that you don't want begging, then it's just a matter of time before you have Konrad resigned to the fact that the party is over, at least at the dinner table.

When Konrad is steady enough to do the LONG DOWN away from your side during dinner, then establish his "place" where he stays while you eat. He should be put in his place every evening while you are eating, and praised when you release him at the end of the meal. It won't be too long before you will be eating dinner in the company of a well-trained, well-behaved dog lying quietly in the corner.

To cure a begging problem:

1)   Do not feed your dog from the table.

2)   Place your dog on a LONG DOWN by your side during dinner. Be prepared to reinforce the command.

3)   As your dog becomes steadier on the LONG DOWN, teach him to remain in his place during dinner.

4)   Be sure to release him at the end of the meal with lots of praise.

Jumping

Dogs jump on people as a form of greeting. They start doing this in an attempt to get close to the person's mouth. This is because one of the ways in which dogs greet each other is by licking the lips and mouth of a returning pack member.

There are really two rewards for the dog who jumps. The first is that he is greeting you, or attempting to, as he wants, by getting close to your mouth. The second reward, and the one that keeps the dog jumping even though you've tried "everything" to get him to stop, is that in the process of putting him back down on the floor, you pet and give him lots of physical contact. Your tone may be angry, but your hands are petting and rewarding.

If you have a puppy that doesn't jump on you and you want to prevent him from starting, crouch down to greet your puppy in a calm and unexcited manner so that he doesn't learn to get overexcited when you come home. From the beginning, teach your puppy to sit for your greeting, and stroke him briefly—about five seconds—in that position.

If you have a dog who is already jumping, you have to decide if you sincerely want to stop the behavior. Remember, you can't allow Konrad to jump on *you,* and expect him to know better than to jump on your mother-in-law, who doesn't like him anyway. Konrad can't tell the difference between people who don't mind the jumping and those who do. He can learn not to jump at all, or he will jump whenever it's appropriate to *him.*

Having made up your mind that you don't want Konrad to jump on you or anyone else anymore, you can put a stop to this behavior.

To stop your dog from jumping on you:

1) When you come home, ignore your dog. Walk right past him, saying nothing to him even if he's jumping on you.

2) When you are out of the entry area, you may greet your dog as follows:

> Tell him to "Sit" and, while he is sitting, briefly and calmly pet and talk to him for 5 seconds. Initially, you may have to place him in a sit, but do so quickly and with a minimum of touching. When you pet him, crouch down rather than standing erect over him

3) After you have greeted him for five seconds, go on about your business and ignore him for a while longer.

4) Train your dog on a regular basis, paying special attention to the LONG DOWN exercise.

To stop your dog from jumping on other people:

1) Before letting people in the door, tell your dog to "Sit" and have him remain in position until you release him. Initially, you may have to put on his leash and collar to enforce this command.

2) Have your visitors ignore the dog, walk to the room you will be in, and sit down.

3) Heel your dog into that room, and have him do a LONG DOWN by your chair for ten or 15 minutes. If he is quiet, release him, but if he is not, keep him on a LONG DOWN until he is.

The cure for jumping requires practice and repetition. We recommend that you spend a weekend setting up a training situation to teach your dog not to jump on people any more. Plan it like a day-long party. Ask your friends and relatives to come at scheduled, staggered times during the day, offering them food and drink in return for their help in training your dog. After several repetitions with different people, your dog will be more willing to sit still when people come to visit. The more you repeat this exercise, the easier it will become. In a short time, you will be able to have your dog sit quietly on command while you greet guests.

Chewing

There are several reasons that dogs chew. One is a physiological need connected with teething. When puppies reach a certain age, they *must* chew. If they don't have anything to chew on, they'll find something—even doors and walls. This need peaks around six to ten months of age.

Another reason dogs chew is that their owners have given them personal items to have as toys—old bath towels, slippers, socks, shoes—and the dog has learned that these objects are his own. Dogs cannot tell the difference between the shoes you are no longer interested in wearing and the expensive dress shoes you just bought.

Often a well-meaning dog owner will give a puppy such a tremendous variety of toys that the pup cannot differentiate between what is his to chew and what belongs to the rest of the family.

Many dogs chew because they have been permitted to, their owners thinking that this is a stage they are going through and that the pup will outgrow it. Then, because they are permitted to chew, the destruction becomes habitual. One day the owner wakes up and realizes that Konrad is two years old, and this stage should have been over long ago.

Probably, the main reason that dogs chew is because of boredom and frustration. A dog left to his own devices all day may find unacceptable ways to amuse himself. Remember, if a dog is feeling tense and frustrated, he won't hold these feelings in—in this case chewing is his release.

Chewing, unlike jumping, is something that most owners feel consistent about—they don't want their dogs to do it! Chewing is an expensive problem, and when a problem hits us in the pocketbook, it is taken seriously.

The chances are, once again, that you have tried "everything" to get your dog to stop chewing. You've lost your temper, showed him his destruction and hollered, and hit him; you've tried putting evil tasting potions on your possessions; you've tried to be good, to put things away and close doors tight, but you can't live in a fortress, and sometimes you forget. Why doesn't Konrad understand? Is he stupid?

Konrad doesn't understand because your yelling and getting upset is totally removed from the destructive chewing. Here is the probable scenario: You leave for work at eight o'clock, after having checked most of your possessions to make sure they are put away or out of Konrad's reach. Just before you close the door, you admonish Konrad not to touch anything—to be good. You use your firmest, most threatening voice, and Konrad, who doesn't understand your language, is left alone with the feeling that something is very wrong. This immediately creates tension for him, who hasn't yet done anything worth yelling about.

So now you're gone. Konrad, who likes to imitate you, goes around the house and checks things out, as you did. Then he finds something that feels particularly good to him, and he sets about playing with it.

It is now nine o'clock, and Konrad is beginning to work over your new shoe. He plays with it, nibbles on it, and tosses it around, having a wonderful time. He leaves it for a while to rest, and later comes back to it for more fun, spending much of his day having a terrific time with your new shoe.

Five o'clock arrives, when you return from work and, lo and behold, the first thing you see is your brand new shoe. At least you *think* it's your new shoe, but it's beyond recognition now so it's hard to tell. You grab Konrad by the collar, push his face into the shoe, and yell and even hit him to let him know how awful you think he is for chewing your shoe.

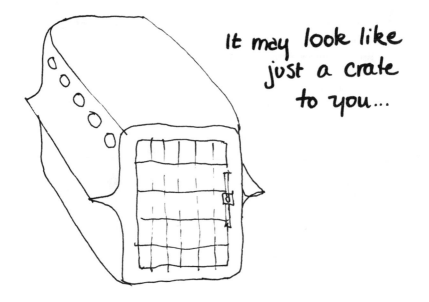

It may look like just a crate to you...

but to a dog it quickly becomes home...

Can you convince Konrad by this that chewing your shoe was terrible? It *wasn't* terrible. It was a great deal of fun. Konrad spent the better part of the day with your shoe and never once did anything try to discourage him from chewing it. What was bad today was not his chewing the shoe, but your coming home. If you had stayed away, the shoe chewing would have remained a wonderful event.

All you are doing by chastising Konrad in this situation is making your homecoming unpleasant and frightening. It will not stop him from chewing your shoes in the future, but it will make him fear you. So what can you do to stop Konrad from chewing?

Chewing is one behavior problem for which the prevention and the cure are the same. We believe in confinement when a dog is left alone. Confinement puts the dog in an environment where he can do no wrong. He can have a toy, such as a marrow bone, to fulfill his physiological need to chew, but he will have access to nothing else that he can destroy.

Think about what it is you want your dog to do while you are away all day. You want him to chew *his* toys, to rest and relax, and to greet you happily when you come home. You don't want him to chew your possessions. You don't want him to race around the house and knock things off tables. You don't want him to empty the garbage, let the feathers out of your pillows, or strew toilet paper around the living room. Confinement prevents him from doing all these things.

Confinement may be in a small, well-ventilated room such as a bathroom or utility room. If you already have a chewing problem this may be too large an area. We strongly advocate crating dogs. A crate is a wire cage in which there is enough room for your dog to stand up, turn around, and lie down comfortably. Crating a dog keeps him out of mischief so that when you come home you can greet him happily without having to clean up that day's destruction.

From your dog's point of view, the crate becomes his den, his refuge, a place where he can relax and rest. A crate becomes to a dog what a den is to his ancestor, the wolf—a place where they can fully let down their guards and relax.

In the case of a young puppy, we strongly recommend starting it off in a crate to avoid any unpleasant habits from forming. It takes no time at all before he will run into his crate on command, and won't mind staying there until he is let out. This also greatly facilitates housetraining. Even older dogs quickly get used to being crated.

We look upon crating a dog in the same light as putting a child in a playpen or crib. When you are free to watch the child, he can have freedom within the house. But if you are unable to watch the child or puppy, it is preferable to put him in a safe environment. For information on Crate Training, see Chapter 3, "You and Your Dog."

If your dog is barking from boredom and frustration...

obedience train him and make him
an integral part of the family...

To solve a chewing problem:

1) Recognize your dog's physiological need to chew. Make sure he has one chewable toy of his own.

2) Provide him with no more than one toy. That one is his; everything else is yours.

3) Keep your chewable objects out of your dog's reach.

4) Confine him in a small area, preferably a crate, when you are unable to keep an eye on him.

5) Train him on a regular basis. This will give him a function and make him a contributing member of the household.

Once your dog has become accustomed to chewing only his own toy, you may then begin to give him more freedom. When you are no longer confining your dog, observe the following rules:

1) Be sure all chewable objects are kept out of his reach.

2) Do not rush around the house just before you leave frantically stashing things away. This kind of manic behavior can cause anxiety or excitement in your dog. Also, he may mimic your behavior after you leave.

3) Prior to leaving the house, sit down quietly for five minutes. Read the paper, listen to the radio, have a cup of coffee, but do not pay attention to your dog.

4) When it is time to leave, get up and leave. Be unemotional. No teary goodbyes. No "Mummy will miss you, but she'll be back soon." No admonitions to "be good." Simply leave.

5) Should your dog regress, go back to confinement for a short time, while you examine the possible causes of the relapse. Is there a crisis in the family? Did you lose your job? Have you failed to follow our advice?

Barking

Persistent, uncontrollable barking is not only a nuisance to you, but to your neighbors as well. In order to approach a solution to the problem, it is necessary to have an understanding of what is causing your dog's barking. Is he doing it because he is a good watchdog? Is he barking because there is a strange dog on his property? Is he tied up in the yard and ignored and therefore barking out of boredom? Does he bark to get attention in the house?

If your dog is barking as an alert to let you know that someone or something is on the property, he is doing what comes naturally. Dogs feel protective of their territory, and their barking, as a warning to an intruder or to alert you that someone is there, is instinctive. Most people want their dogs to bark under these circumstances, and even encourage it with praise. In this case it is not the barking that is the problem. It is that the dog won't stop barking when you want him to.

Some dogs bark to get attention. There are some breeds that are more prone to this behavior than others. Shelties, Collies and many toy dogs are notorious barkers. Your attention is their reward, so this is a self-perpetuating problem. You can't ignore that piercing bark, yet to pay attention is to reward the behavior.

The most common reason for dogs barking continuously is boredom and frustration. Barking is their outlet, and the reward is the release of tension. When a dog is isolated and begins barking, the result is that the owner comes running out of the house to scold him. For just a moment, the dog is not alone. His owner is with him, relieving his boredom and loneliness. Sure he's being scolded but, to a lonely dog, having someone with him who's yelling is better than not having anyone at all. To a dog left alone too much, the owner's presence, even when angry, is a reward.

Barking that results from isolation can be both prevented and cured by not putting your dog in the frustrating position of being left alone in the yard too long. Both the prevention and the cure for a barking problem of this nature are to obedience train your dog regularly. This gives him a job to do so he is performing a function, and it makes him an integral part of the family by bringing him in the house.

If you do not have him in the house because of other problems, solve them. Dogs who bark because of isolation, and dogs who dig for the same reason (see next section), cannot be broken by any magical cure. If you have a dog with a problem resulting from his frustration, the only cure involves your spending some time with your dog and making him a member of the family.

When the dog does his duty as a watchdog by barking to alert you, it is commendable behavior. But when he keeps it up longer than necessary, you have a problem. To teach him to quiet down once he has alerted you, use the positive approach to modify this behavior as follows:

1) Follow the lesson plans to teach him to respond to your command to "COME."

2) Once he is responding, use this command when he is barking at something. You may have to use food as a reward to get him away from the window or door, but whatever it takes, call him to you, reward him with food and praise, and take control of the situation.

3) Thank him for letting you know that someone or something is out there, and give him a DOWN command. Praise and leave him on a DOWN-STAY.

4) Go to the window/door to see what was there, return to your dog, praise him for staying and release him. If the window/door he was barking at is in a different room, take him to that room, tell him DOWN-STAY and proceed as above.

5) If he immediately runs back to resume his barking after your

release, call him to you again, repeat the procedure, and then do a LONG DOWN for ten minutes.

What you are doing is teaching your dog that it is good for him to alert you to danger, that he should come to you to tell you about it, but then you take over. You are in control of both the situation and your dog. He learns that his job is done once he lets you know that there is something out there.

If your dog is barking, do not yell at him. At best, your yelling will be interpreted by your dog as your joining in with him. At worst, you will be yelling at him for following a natural instinct. This will confuse him and may undermine your relationship.

Barking in the Crate

If you are confining your dog to a crate and he begins barking to be let out, you have a special problem. You must not let your dog out of the crate when he is barking, or you will be rewarding his barking. He will associate his barking with freedom and will continue to make noise in the future when he wants to get out of the crate. Therefore, before you let your dog out of the crate, he must be quiet.

To stop your dog from barking in the crate, and to teach him to respond to the command "QUIET," take half a glass of water and throw it directly in his face as you say "QUIET!" After he has been quiet, let him out of the crate. Gradually increase the length of time that your dog must remain quiet before being let out. Initially, it may only be a second or two, but you should be able to have quiet for a minute or more after your command before letting him out of the crate. After several repetitions with the glass of water, just saying "QUIET" should be enough to have him stop barking.

Digging

Digging is a behavior problem with many possible causes. The rewards in most cases are apparent, once you understand the reasons behind the digging. In some digging cases, prevention is more difficult than in others, but it is necessary to have an understanding of *why* your dog is digging in order to undertake a program to deal with it.

Digging is instinctive for some dogs. Instinctive digging can occur for several reasons.

* Terriers and terrier mixes have been bred for generations to dig. This is instinctive behavior, and the reward is the satisfaction of that instinct. You probably cannot prevent this digging unless you cover your yard with Astroturf or green cement.

* Pregnant bitches will dig to make a nest in which to have their puppies. If you provide your pregnant female with a whelping box with rags or newspaper to dig into and tear up, you can generally channel this behavior so that it is not destructive. You cannot prevent her digging to nest. To do

DOGS dig for many reasons...

but the most common is BOREDOM!

so would be cruel. If it upsets you, don't breed your female.

* Dogs will dig to bury bones. This is instinctive caching behavior. While not all dogs will bury bones, if yours is one that does—and you don't like his doing it—don't give him bones.

* Another reason for digging is when a dog is hot. He will find a nice shady spot and try to dig down to some damp earth to lie on. It's cooler there, and that is quite rewarding. In many cases you can prevent this digging by providing your dog with a cool environment. Some dogs will wet themselves in a kiddy pool and then lie in the shade without digging up the soil.

* Many dogs like to mimic their owners. When they watch you digging in the garden, they want to try it too. This is instinctive, and its satisfaction is rewarding. Preventing this type of digging is simply to keep your dog away from the yard when you are gardening. Leave him in the house where he can't see what you are doing, and he won't be tempted to emulate you.

* Some dogs that are penned up try to dig out of the pen. Their freedom is the reward.

* The most common causes of digging are boredom, frustration and loneliness. If a dog is isolated in the yard for hours on end, he will take out his frustrations in any way he can. This often means digging—usually near the house, by the stairs, or around the foundation. The reward is the release of tension. Remember, dogs don't hold back their emotions—they let it all out.

We know that not many people reading this book would care to employ their dogs to excavate for an addition on the house or search for oil in the backyard. Holes are not something we like to have around. However, if your dog's digging problem is caused by instinctual behavior, you will continue to have a digging problem if you leave your dog unattended in the yard for any length of time.

Even if you catch him in the act of digging, and scold him at that time, while your dog may understand that digging makes you angry, the rewards involved are so strong that his instincts will probably override his awareness of your displeasure. Dogs do not dig out of spite or because they know it is wrong and want to teach you a lesson.

To cure the problem of digging by a dog who is bored and frustrated, don't put your dog in the position of being isolated and ignored. These situations often lead to psychological problems.

Making your dog a part of the family, giving him a function, and teaching him to be a contributing member of the household will prevent and cure a digging problem. To give your dog a function, train him on a regular basis. Exercise him so that he is not physically tense. If the reason you keep him in the yard is that you don't like his behavior in the house, train him and work on the specific problems so that he can be an integral

The pack leader gets first pick of the choicest foods and so forth...

However, follow the behavior modification program and you'll find most dogs are willing to relinquish pack leadership...

BIG CHEESE

part of your household.

To cure a digging problem:

1) Identify the underlying cause of the problem.
2) Don't keep your dog isolated in the yard.
3) Obedience train your dog every day.
4) Make your dog a contributing member of the household and give him a function.

Above all, do not try to chastise your dog by showing him the holes and yelling.

Biting

Biting is a special behavior problem. There are any number of causes for a dog to bite, and if your problem is severe, we suggest that you consult with a dog behavior specialist in your area. In this section we will cover the most common reason for biting: an attempt to dominate the pack and be pack leader. You may think your dog is biting because you tried to take a bone or a Kleenex away from him, he got in the garbage and you yelled, or you tried to get him off the couch. But, as you will see, these are all related to lack of leadership on your part.

Most dogs are not that eager to have the responsibility of pack leadership and will take over only in the absence of your leadership. Along with the responsibilities of taking control of the pack go these perquisites: the pack leader sleeps where he wants, eats the choicest food, and owns all the pack possessions, from bones to dirty Kleenex.

You may not particularly mind if your dog is the pack leader, but you can't have it both ways. You cannot allow your dog to be pack leader part of the time, then one day decide that you've had enough and try to take over the leadership in the space of 30 seconds. If you allow your dog to dominate your pack, then he is in control. So, when the time comes that you try to get him off your bed so you can get in, he may bite you. Or if you find he has removed the roast from the counter and you try to take it back, he may bite you. Or if you find him chewing your shoes and you try to take them from him, he may bite you.

In dog terms, this isn't wrong. If you have allowed your dog to become pack leader, from his point of view you are wrong when you suddenly challenge that leadership.

But this situation can be prevented. Attempts at leadership usually begin at about 13 weeks of age. At the time your dog first attempts to dominate you, if you handle the situation properly, it will all be over in a matter of days or, in the case of a really strong-willed and dominant dog, weeks.

At this age, not before, when your puppy bites you, even in play, or if he takes the leash in his mouth when you are training him, you must deal with it immediately and firmly.

During training, when your pup takes the leash in his mouth, use your right hand to quickly and firmly pull it through his mouth in a firm check toward the right. This will generally cause the snap of the leash to knock against his mouth at the same time he is checked. As you do this, say "STOP IT!" in a firm, stern voice. Immediately give your puppy a HEEL command, and begin walking briskly. Praise him for being at heel. If he takes the leash in his mouth again, repeat the check while you continue walking. After several repetitions of this, your pup will stop trying to take the leash in his mouth—for the time being. That doesn't mean his attempt to test your leadership is over, but it will usually end temporarily.

If your puppy tries to bite you instead of the leash, take the loop end of the leash and smack him across the top of his muzzle while saying "STOP IT!" Do not follow this with praise.

In addition to dealing with this overt attempt to dominate you, your training must include special emphasis on the exercise designed to teach your dog that you are the pack leader: the LONG DOWN. If you have an especially dominant puppy, one who repeatedly is testing you by taking the leash in his mouth, coming back again and again to bite your hands or nipping at your ankles while you heel, then include five LONG DOWNS each week instead of the three that we recommend for most people.

If you have an older dog who is already dominating you and growls at you or even tries to bite you in situations like those described above, the cure is to concentrate on becoming the pack leader through training and doing some behavior modification exercises. Follow the training program in this book. This will teach your dog in a positive manner that you are in control. In addition to this, the following rules must be adhered to at all times.

1)   Absolutely no food treats unless the dog has had to work for it—to perform a function or obey a command such as "Sit" or "Down." Do not give him any between meal snacks.

2)   Pet your dog for only five seconds at a time, and only after the dog has been made to respond to a command such as "SIT." Do not pet and stroke for minutes on end.

3)   If your dog nudges your arm to be petted, you must make him respond to a command such as "Sit" before petting him, and then pet him for no more than five seconds.

4)   When you stop petting him after five seconds, say "NO MORE" or "ENOUGH" or some other command word used consistently, fold your arms, and ignore the dog. Never resume petting your dog once you have said "NO MORE" until after a lapse of ten minutes.

5)   Do not allow your dog to precede you through doorways or up or down stairs. Get into the habit of giving him a firm "STAY" command, go

214

through the doorway or up or down the stairs and then release him from the stay command and give verbal praise.

6)   Give your dog only one toy to play with. Everything else is yours.

7)   Do not play any games with him except fetch and, during this game, he must bring the object back to you and release it on command. If this means you must keep him on a long line initially, so be it.

8)   Train your dog regularly and consistently. Even after your 8-week program is completed, set aside a regular time—five to ten minutes is usually sufficient—for some obedience work twice a week.

9)   Concentrate on doing LONG DOWNS five days a week during the initial training program, and three days each week thereafter. You can do them while you're eating dinner, so they don't require any special time.

10)   When you groom your dog—trim nails or brush—he must stand, sit, or lie still while you brush him. Work with him for short periods of time to enforce his allowing you to do this.

11)   When you sweep or vacuum the floor, or your dog is lying in front of a cabinet door or doorway to which you need access, make him move. Do not work around him. You, as the pack leader, have the right to go anywhere in the territory. The other pack members must get out of the way.

This approach to taking over pack leadership does not involve your confronting your dog in any physical battles or using any kind of force to "show him who's boss." We prefer this method because it teaches the dog, in canine terms, that you are now in control. Dogs are not unwilling to relinquish the pack leadership to another pack member who deserves it, and it can be done without fights or bloodshed. You can take over your own pack if you approach the situation in the way we have outlined.

Car Sickness

Very few dogs suffer from true motion sickness. In most cases, a dog who gets carsick (which may range from excessive drooling to vomiting) has developed a negative association with riding in the car. It is likely that the dog who gets carsick doesn't go for many rides other than to the veterinarian. We might compare his reaction to that of a child who, everytime he gets in the car, goes to the doctor for a shot. It wouldn't take long before that child, or your dog, associates the car with an unpleasant occurrence.

To prevent this make sure you take your puppy for frequent, short, pleasant rides ending in play. If he does get sick, don't reinforce the behavior by giving him a lot of attention, stroking and solicitous talk. That kind of response from you tends to reinforce the dog's reaction, rather than alleviate it.

If you already have a problem with your dog getting carsick, the

Be patient while gradually getting your dog used to the car, and maintain a light happy demeano

following program of desensitization will benefit you both.

1) Open all the doors to your car with the engine turned off, and coax your dog into it. At the same time, use a command, like "Get in the car," said in a happy tone. If your dog won't get in on his own, place him in the car.

Once in, offer him a tidbit, laugh and talk happily to him, and immediately let him out of the car. Repeat this five times. You should notice that your dog is becoming less reluctant to get into the car. Repeat this until your dog willingly gets in on your command. Remember to keep laughing and offering treats.

2) Once your dog is getting into the car willingly, close the doors on one side, engine still off, and repeat the above. If he shows apprehension, continue to work on this step until he is relaxed again. Keep laughing and giving treats.

3) When he is comfortable at step two, tell your dog to get in the car, give him a treat, and close all the doors. Laugh and talk to him and give him another treat. If he shows apprehension at this stage, repeat it until he is calm.

4) Tell your dog to get in the car, close the car doors and turn on the engine. Don't go anywhere yet. Give your dog a treat, laugh and talk to him, and turn off the engine. Repeat until he is comfortable then move on to the next step.

5) Get in the car with your dog, give him a treat and take him for a *short* drive, a quarter of a mile or less, and return home. Take your dog out of the car and play with him. Make the game lots of fun, including lots of laughter.

6) Gradually lengthen the trips you take, always beginning them with a treat for getting in the car and ending them with a play session.

Throughout this remedial exercise, your attitude and tone of voice are critical. You must maintain a light and happy demeanor. At no time should you act concerned about your dog's behavior. Avoid a sympathetic tone of voice and solicitous phrases like, "It's a-a-ll r-i-i-i-ght. Don't worry. Nothing's going to hurt you." This kind of concern conveys itself to your dog as apprehension on your part. Since he doesn't understand your words, and only can pick up your emotional state, what he gets out of this is that you are apprehensive about the car ride too. Therefore, there really must be something to throw up about. To overcome this, use lots of laughter and have a very happy attitude.

It is more common for dogs to experience car sickness in vans, where they can't see out of a window, than in a regular car. Desensitization in such a case should be undertaken in a car and continued in the van.

Coprophagy

Halitosis is one thing, but no one wants to be greeted by his canine companion who is in the habit of eating stools.

The most common causes of stool eating are dietary deficiencies— usually poor protein assimilation—the precise cause of which will have to be established by your veterinarian. It is also caused by boredom and, once started, can develop into an annoying habit. Some dogs seem to take a particular delight in frozen stools.

With proper treatment, the dog will stop by himself. If it has become a habit, the cure is quite simple, as demonstrated by the following incident.

Mary had trained both her dogs with us. About a year after she called to say, "My dogs are eating their stools. I have consulted my veterinarian, and the food supplements he prescribed did not help. I then went to a dog psychiatrist and he told me to sprinkle tabasco sauce on the stools. That stopped the dogs for a while, but now they have developed a taste for tabasco and are right back at it again. I don't know what to do anymore."

We advised Mary that while she was out in the yard sprinkling tabasco, it would probably be just as easy to clean up after the dogs, thereby precluding the dogs from doing their own cleaning up. Two weeks later she called again and excitedly exclaimed, "It works—they are no longer eating their stools!" Moral of the story: keep the yard cleaned.

13

Obedience Trials

ALMOST EVERY WEEKEND of the year thousands of dog fanciers pack their picnic lunches, throw little Konrad and all his paraphernalia into their cars and head for the dog show. For some it is a business, for some it is a sport, and for some it is a leisure activity.

For the true aficionado, showing his dog is a true challenge. During the week he plans his strategy and painstakingly prepares for the weekend. His vehicle is always ready—maps, a compass, a lawn chair, his trusty C.B. and three sets of rain gear. He will need all of these since dog shows are invariably held in next to impossible to find locations, and it frequently rains. If held indoors, which happens in some parts of the country, the building is either too hot or too cold, always too noisy, and you can never find the bathroom.

You may have gathered by now that dog shows are never perfect unless, of course, you win. There is always plenty to complain about, the favorite topic being the state of judging. When you don't win, the judge is obviously blind, feeble-minded or bought off. This attitude has led to a sort of love-hate relationship between exhibitors—bosom buddies one weekend and bitter enemies the next, depending on who won. Like any other leisure activity, there is a certain amount of irrationality about it. You may ask "Why do people do it?" The answer to that is decidedly beyond the scope of this book.

The governing body of all this is the American Kennel Club (AKC) which registers pure-bred dogs, approves judges and keeps track of the

TRUE AFICIONADOS OF DOG SHOWS
ARE EASILY RECOGNIZED...

Taking Konrad to a Dog Show.

results of dog shows. To enter Konrad in a dog show, he must be registered with the American Kennel Club.

You can exhibit Konrad either in obedience trials or conformation shows. When you exhibit in conformation, Konrad will be judged solely on how well the judge thinks he conforms to the official AKC standard for his particular breed. Among the items considered by the judge are Konrad's size, color, structure and movement.

When you exhibit Konrad at an obedience trial he will be judged on how well he performs certain predetermined obedience exercises. Most dog shows are combined conformation shows and obedience trials so that you can enter Konrad in either conformation or obedience or both.

Exhibiting a dog in obedience trials is a good excuse to get out of the house and have some fun. It also lets you show off Konrad's training and earn obedience titles. The American Kennel Club awards obedience titles to dogs who have successfully completed the requirements for a C.D. or a C.D.X. or a U.D. or an O.T.Ch. Titles are awarded by the AKC to dogs who earn three qualifying scores in each respective class under three different judges at AKC approved trials.

The initials C.D. stand for Companion Dog. The exercises the dog is required to perform in the Novice Class for this title are: Heel on Leash (including a Figure 8), Stand for Examination, Heel Off Leash, Recall, Sit Stay for 1 minute and Down-Stay for 3 minutes. In order to get a qualifying score, called a *leg,* the dog must pass each exercise with more than half the point value assigned to that exercise and obtain a total score of at least 170 out of 200 points.

The initials C.D.X. stand for Companion Dog Excellent. The exercises in the Open Class that the dog is required to perform for the C.D.X. title are: Heel Off Leash (including a Figure 8), Drop on Recall, Retrieve on the Flat, Retrieve Over High Jump, a three-minute Sit-Stay and five-minute Down-Stay with the handler out of sight.

The initials U.D. stand for Utility Dog. The exercises in the Utility Class are: Signal Exercise, Scent Discrimination, Directed Retrieve, Directed Jumping and a group Stand for Examination.

The initials O.T.Ch. stand for Obedience Trial Champion. This title is awarded to outstanding dogs who have completed their Utility Dog title and continue to win in competition.

If you are interested in the specific requirements for these titles, contact the American Kennel Club at 51 Madison Avenue, New York, New York 10010 for a free copy of the *Obedience Regulations.*

It is necessary to enter trials ahead of time. The closing date for such entries is usually 2 to 3 weeks before the date of the trial and late entries are not accepted. The announcement of an upcoming trial containing the date of the trial, closing date for entries, location, classes and judges is called a

"Premium List." The Premium List also contains an official entry blank to enter the trial.

The Premium List of an upcoming trial can be obtained by writing to the Trial Secretary of the club conducting the trial or, if the trial is handled by a Superintendent, from the Superintendent. Announcements of upcoming trials, as well as the addresses of the Trial Secretaries or Superintendents are contained in *PURE-BRED DOGS, The American Kennel Gazette,* the official publication of the American Kennel Club, and other dog publications.

Obedience trials are held throughout the year, usually on Saturdays and Sundays. They can be held either indoors or outdoors.

Before actually entering a trial, it is a good idea to enter several *matches.* A match is a practice trial which is conducted in much the same manner as a regular trial but a qualifying score at a match does not count toward an AKC obedience title. The purpose of a match is to see whether or not Konrad is ready to enter a real trial. It also affords you an opportunity to learn the mechanics and intricacies of exhibiting your dog. Usually your dog may be entered on the day of the match and, unless it is an AKC Sanctioned Match, mixed breeds and non-AKC-registered dogs may be entered.

Most matches have a class called Beginners or Sub-Novice in which all the exercises are performed on leash. This class is not offered at a trial. If you are not certain how your dog will react under battle conditions, or if you are not quite sure of his off-leash work, you should enter him in this class.

If you have followed the lessons in this book and have successfully trained your dog to perform the exercises in these eight lessons, your dog knows all the exercises required for the C.D. title. If you are interested in obedience trials, contact your local kennel club or obedience club for further information.

14

Synopsis of Training Progressions

About-Turn in Place *Chapter*

1   Sit dog in heel position; gather leash short in right hand.   4
Place left hand close to leash snap. Keep both hands in
front of your legs and close together. With "Konrad, Heel"
take two steps straight forward, turn in place away from
dog 180° to face in the opposite direction, and take two
more steps forward. Say "sit" and place dog in a sit at heel.

2   Take one step forward, turn away from dog 180°, take one   6
step forward, and sit dog.

Automatic Sit

1   Place your right hand on dog's chest, left hand on withers.   4
As you stop, say "sit" and tuck dog into sit as for Sequence
1 of Sit. Keep body facing straight ahead and line dog up
next to your left thigh.

2   With rings of collar at top of dog's neck—as you begin to   5 & 6
come to a halt, grasp leash snap with right hand. Check upward with right hand as you tuck dog into a sit with left
hand. Say "sit."

3   With rings of collar at top of dog's neck—as you prepare to   7, 8 & 9
     stop, grasp leash close to snap with left hand. Keeping left
     forearm parallel with dog's spine, check straight up with
     left hand as you say "sit." If he begins to sit crookedly, say
     "heel" and take a step forward. Position him as in Sequence
     2.

4   Do three Automatic Sits as in Sequence 3, then do two   10
     checking upward with left hand but do not say "sit."

5   Do three Automatic Sits, checking upward as you come to   11
     a halt, but do not say "sit." Then do two Automatic Sits
     without checking.

Down

1   Place your right hand behind dog's right foreleg, palm   4
     open and facing away from dog, thumb in palm. Reach
     across his back with your left arm, place left hand behind
     his left foreleg. Say "down" as you lift the front end and
     lower dog to the ground.

2   Place left hand on dog's withers and hold object of attrac-   5
     tion in your right hand in front of dog's head, just above his
     eye level. Bring right hand quickly down and out to a point
     in front of dog as you say "down." Give object as a reward.

3   Seat dog and kneel in front, holding object in right hand,   6
     leash folded in left hand. Place two fingers of left hand in
     dog's collar under his neck. Say "down" and move object
     downward. Apply downward pressure with left hand in
     collar.

4   With dog sitting at left side, fold leash into your left hand.   9
     Place two fingers of left hand in collar, palm down. Com-
     mand "down" and, if dog fails to respond, apply downward
     pressure with left hand in collar.

Down Hand Signal

1   Kneel on one knee in front of dog. Fold leash into left hand   7
     and place two fingers of left hand in dog's collar under muz-
     zle. Raise arm straight up, command "down" and push
     back and down with left hand. Keep arm in signal position
     as you praise.

2   From 3 feet in front of dog, kneel on one knee. Give signal 8
and command "down." If necessary, grasp leash snap with
left hand and check downward. Leave arm erect as you
praise.

3   Stand erect 3 feet in front as you give the command and 9
signal twice, then try signal alone with no voice command.
If dog fails to respond, step toward dog and check straight
down with left hand.

4   Stand 6 feet in front of dog as you give signal and voice 10
command. If dog doesn't respond, step toward him and
check straight down with left hand, keeping right arm erect.
Do twice with voice/signal, and then two times with signal
only.

Down-Stay

1   Down your dog at your left side, command/signal "stay" 6
and go 3 feet in front. Begin with a one-minute stay before
pivoting back. Work up to a three-minute Down-Stay.

2   From 3 feet in front, do a one-minute Down-Stay. Pivot 7
back.

3   From 6 feet in front, do a one-minute Down-Stay and work 8
up to a three-minute Down-Stay. Return around behind.

4   From 6 feet in front, work on one-minute Down-Stays on 9
different surfaces.

5   Do a one-minute Down-Stay from 6 feet in front, then re- 10
turn around behind to heel position, pause, drop leash,
command "stay," and go 6 feet in front again. Remain in
front for 2 minutes.

6   As you increase distance, decrease time. Begin 10 feet away 11
for 1 minute. Work up to a three-minute Down-Stay at 10
feet, then go 15 feet away for 1 minute and work up to 3
minutes at that distance. Work up to a three-minute Down-
Stay at 20 feet.

Finish

1   Leave dog on Sit-Stay and step directly in front of him, toe- 8
to-toe. Fold leash into right hand and place left hand near

snap of leash, palm down, under dog's muzzle. Keep hands close together. Command "Konrad, Heel" and walk straight ahead, three or four steps past your dog, and place him into a sit at heel.

2 Stand in front of your sitting dog, holding leash short in both hands, keeping hands close together. Command "Konrad, Heel," take two steps backward as you turn dog toward you in a counterclockwise direction, then take two steps forward guiding him into heel position with "sit." 9

3 Stand in front of dog and hold leash as above. Place left foot way out to the side and behind you. Say, "Konrad, Heel," and guide dog into heel position as you bring your left foot even with right. Sit dog at heel. 10

4 Stand in front of dog and hold leash as above. Say, "Konrad, Heel," and move your left foot out to the side and behind you as you guide him into heel position. 11

5 Stand in front of dog, command "Konrad, Heel." If he does not move to heel position himself, firmly check in the same direction you were guiding in Sequence 4. Keep feet stationary. 11

Heeling on Leash

1 Throw the leash across your chest and over your right shoulder. Sit dog at heel. Call dog's name, followed by "Heel" and begin walking at a brisk pace. When dog strays from heel position, use left hand to check him back to position, praise immediately, and quickly take hand off the leash. Practice until you can heel for 10 paces in a straight line without checking dog. 4

2 Practice heeling until you can walk for 15 paces in a straight line and make two about turns without checking dog and with no tension on the leash. 5

Circles

Circles are 4 feet in diameter, leash held in control position. For Circle Left, keep dog in heel position as you circle toward the left, walking very slowly. For Circle Right, keep dog at heel as you circle to the right at a trot. 5

3   Practice heeling until you can walk for 20 paces, do an 6
about-turn, and walk for another 20 paces with no tension
on the leash.

Changes of Pace

Change pace gradually so you are moving very slowly, 6
walk for 10 steps at a slow pace, then change pace gradually back to a brisk, normal pace. For the Fast pace, change
gradually to speed up to a trot, trot for steps, then gradually slow down to normal again. Practice changes of pace
until you can move at the Fast and Slow paces with no tension on the leash for 10 steps.

4   Begin each day's session with a two-minute heeling drill. 7
Incorporate changes of pace and circles. Be enthusiastic
and animated. Enjoy yourself and your dog will enjoy this
too.

Left Turn in Place

1   Place left foot in front of dog's feet at a 90° angle. With 10
"Konrad, Heel" take a large step with your right foot and
close with your left.

2   Place left foot in front of dog's feet at a 90° angle. With 11
"Konrad, Heel" take a small step beyond your left foot with
your right, and close with your left.

Long Down

1   Sit on floor beside dog. Place him down using command 4
"down." Replace him as necessary as he gets up, or prevent his getting up by placing hand on withers. Remain on
floor with him for 30 minutes. At end of that time, praise
and release. Practice three times.

2   Place dog in down and sit in chair by his side. Dog is to 5
remain down by chair for 30 minutes. At end, praise and
release. Practice three times.

3   Place dog in down and sit in a chair across the room. Prac- 6
tice 3 times for 30 minutes each.

4   Place dog in down position for 30 minutes. You may move 7
around the room, but don't go out of sight. Practice three
times.

Long Sit

1 Sit dog by your chair for 10 minutes. At end of that time,   5
   praise and release. Repeat three times.

2 Sit dog and you sit in chair across room from him. After 10   6
   minutes, praise and release. Repeat three times.

3 Sit dog and you move around room while he remains sitting   7
   still for 10 minutes. Don't leave room. At end, praise and
   release.

Off-Leash Heeling

1 Position leash for slip release. Command "Konrad, Heel"   5
   and begin to circle left. As you enter circle, release dog.
   Complete circle and stop, sitting dog by placing right hand
   against his chest and tucking him into a sit.

2 Position leash for slip release. Command "Konrad, Heel,"   6
   begin to circle left, and release. Come out of circle at a normal pace and continue for five steps. Stop and sit dog as in
   Sequence 1.

3 Position leash for slip release. Command "Konrad, Heel,"   7
   begin to circle left, and release. Come out of circle at a normal pace and continue for 10 steps. Stop and sit dog as in
   Sequence 1.

4 Position leash for slip release. Heel in a straight line or a   8
   large counterclockwise circle, give Pay Attention check
   and release dog. Do not change pace. Continue heeling for
   20 paces, then stop and sit dog.

5 Give a Pay Attention check before releasing. Tell dog to   9
   "sit" as you come to a halt to have dog do an Automatic
   Sit off leash.

6 Incorporate an About-Turn in Motion with dog off leash.   10
   Call dog's name before turning.

7 Incorporate About-Turn in Motion, Right-Turn and Left-   11
   Turn. Call dog's name as you turn.

Recall

1 Leave dog on Sit-Stay and go 15 feet in front. Turn and   7
   face him. Count to five, kneel down and count to five again.

Place hands on top of thighs, palms up, smile and call "Konrad, Come!" Praise and pet for one full minute.

2   Leave dog on Sit-Stay, count to 10, kneel, count to 10   8
again, place palms up on thighs, smile and call dog. Praise
when he arrives, and while praising place him into a sit in
front of you. Continue praising for one minute.

3   Leave dog on Sit-Stay. Count to 10 before crouching,   9
count to 10 before calling and, as he starts coming toward
you, keep smiling as you stand up. When he arrives in front
of you, reach down to place him in a straight sit in front as
for the Sit in Front. Praise. Tell him "Stay" and walk
around behind to heel position, pause, praise, and release.

4   Leave dog on Sit-Stay, go 15 feet away, turn, count to 10,   10
smile and remain erect as you call. When he gets directly
in front of you, guide him into a Sit in Front. Count to five,
tell him "stay," and return around behind.

5   Repeat as in Sequence 4, but when dog arrives in front of   11
you, tell him to "sit" with no physical guidance. If he begins
to sit crookedly, take two steps backward and guide him
with your hands under his neck in the collar as for the Sit
in Front.

Recall Hand Signal

From 6 feet in front of dog, hold leash in left hand against   10
your chest. Make the hand signal with the right hand
brought up from your right side in an arc, sweeping your
hand across in front of you to slap the leash as you say,
"Konrad, Come." Have him sit straight in front of you with
"sit."

Right Turn in Place

1   Sit dog in heel position and gather leash short in right hand.   4
Place left hand close to leash snap. Keep both hands in
front of your legs and close together. Place right foot at
90° angle, one large step to the right. With "Konrad, Heel"
bring left foot together with right and sit dog.

2   Say, "Konrad, Heel," then take a step to the right and sit   6
your dog.

229

Sit

1   With right hand on dog's chest, left hand at withers, say "sit." Stroke down back and over tail with left hand and tuck into a sit.   4

2   Hold object of attraction in right hand. Say "sit" and bring right hand quickly from in front of dog's head at nose level to a point directly above his head, slightly behind his eyes.   5

3   Kneel in front of dog. Hold object in right hand and make motion from in front of dog's nose to above his head with right hand as you say "sit." Lift dog with left hand in collar if necessary.   6

Sit Hand Signal

1   With dog in down position, stand up in front of him. Fold leash into left hand and place against right hip. Begin signal with right hand, palm open at side, fingers pointing down. Motion back slightly, then forward toward your dog in a sweeping motion upward, slap the leash upward as you bring your hand toward a point directly over dog's head, but don't raise your hand above your waist. Return hand to right side, palm open, as you praise.   7

2   Stand erect 3 feet in front of dog. Hold leash as for Sequence 1. Step toward dog as you slap the leash upward and say "sit." Return hand to your side, palm open, as you praise.   8

3   Repeat as for Sequence 2 two times, and then try signal only without voice command. Continue to slap leash upward as in Sequence 2.   9

4   From 6 feet in front of dog, command/signal Sit. Do two with voice/signal and then two with signal only.   10

Sit in Front

1   Leash off, stand dog and step directly in front. Place two fingers of each hand, palms up, in collar under dog's neck and keep your back straight. Say "sit" and guide dog into a straight sit in front of you. Pivot back to heel to repeat.   8

2   Leave dog on Sit-Stay and go 3 feet in front of him, leash off. Call him with "Konrad, Come." As he arrives in front   9

of you, reach down to guide him into a sit in front as in Sequence 1. Tell him "stay" and back up to repeat.

Sit Stay

1   With rings of collar at back of dog's neck between ears, fold leash into left hand and hold it taut over dog's head, keeping hand below waist. Give signal with right hand, palm brought across body to directly in front of dog's nose. Say "stay" with signal and step directly in front of dog, count to 10, pivot back, pause, praise and release. Work up to a silent count of 30.   5

2   With rings of collar under dog's muzzle, give stay command and signal and move 3 feet in front, then turn and face dog. Position left hand holding leash against midsection with one inch of slack in leash. Place right hand, palm toward dog, under leash midway between the two of you. At the first sign of dog's thinking about moving, step toward dog and slap leash, repeating "stay." Work up to a one-minute Sit-Stay without having to check.   6

Test   With leash on dead ring, incorporate test 3 times each session for 5 to 10 seconds each time. Apply even pressure on the collar, gradually increasing pressure until dog physically resists.   7

3   Repeat as Sequence 2, working up to a two-minute Sit-Stay.   7

4   Test twice, then go 6 feet away from dog. Work up to a two-minute Sit-Stay.   8

5   From 6 feet away, increase time—work up to 3 minutes. Work on different surfaces doing one-minute stays from 6 feet away.   9

6   Do a one-minute Sit-Stay from 6 feet, then return around behind, pause, drop leash by dog's side, repeat "stay," and go 6 feet in front for a count of 10. Work up to a one-minute Sit-Stay with leash dropped next to dog.   10

7   As you increase distance, decrease time. Begin 10 feet away for 10 seconds. Work up to 1 minute at that distance, then go 15 feet away for 10 seconds. Work up to a one-minute stay at 20 feet.   11

Stand

1   Kneel next to your dog facing same direction. Place two   4
fingers of right hand in dog's collar under muzzle, palm
toward floor. Command "stand" and pull forward and
parallel to floor with right hand. Use left hand, palm forward, to apply pressure against the front of the stifles. Keep
dog standing still for 1 minute.

2   Kneel next to dog, facing same direction. With two   5
fingers of right hand in dog's collar under muzzle, command "stand" as you pull forward and parallel to floor. Try
not to touch dog with left hand in front of stifles. Keep dog
standing still for 2 minutes.

Stand For Examination

1   Sit your dog at heel, hold leash in left hand, taut over his   6
head. Command/signal "stay" and remain by his side as a
friend or family member approaches, offers right hand—
palm open to be sniffed—runs hand lightly down dog's
back, and walks away.

2   Leave dog on Sit-Stay and go 3 feet in front as a friend or   7
family member goes over dog as in Sequence 1. Be prepared
to reinforce stay with right hand under leash midway between you.

3   Leave dog on Stand-Stay and go 3 feet in front for 10 sec-   8
onds. Pivot back and methodically examine dog from front
to rear.

4   Stand your dog, leave him on a stay, and stand directly in   9
front of him as a friend or family member goes over him
as in Sequence 1.

5   Stand 3 feet in front of your dog on a Stand-Stay as a friend   10
or family member goes over him as in Sequence 1.

6   Stand 6 feet in front of your dog as a friend or family mem-   11
ber goes over him while he holds a Stand-Stay.

Stand Hand Signal

Place two fingers of your right hand in the collar under   10
dog's muzzle. Hand signal is with left hand, palm open and
parallel to the ground, moved from right to left in front of

dog's eyes. As you give signal/command, take one full step forward with your right leg and close with your left. Keep body facing straight ahead so your dog is standing at heel.

Stand-Stay

1   Position dog in a Stand, leash off. Stand next to dog, say "stay" and remain at his side. Work up to a three-minute Stand-Stay.   6

2   Step directly in front of your standing dog, remain there for 30 seconds, pivot back, pause, praise, and release. Work up to a two-minute Stand-Stay with you right in front.   7

3   Leave dog on Stand-Stay and go 3 feet in front. Remain there without fidgeting and then pivot back to heel position. Pause, praise, and release. Work up to a one-minute Stand-Stay from 3 feet away.   8

4   Leave dog on a Stand-Stay and go 6 feet in front. Work up to a one-minute Stand-Stay. Return around behind. Place two fingers on dog's withers to steady him as you walk behind, then pause, praise, and release.   9

Whistle Training

1   Practice in a room with no distractions. Blow whistle and reward with treat when dog comes. Repeat until dog is responding eagerly to whistle.   5

2   Practice in a confined area outside. Blow whistle and reward/praise dog for coming to you. Practice in three different locations, three times in each.   6

3   Once dog is trained you don't have to reward with a treat every time, but it is best to do so frequently. Continue to practice in confined areas. You will know when dog will reliably come to the whistle when let off leash in an unconfined area.   7

Bibliography

BEHAVIOR

Bergman, Goran, *Why Does Your Dog Do That?* New York: Howell Book House, 1973.

A lucid survey of why a dog behaves in a certain way. Explains the behavior of dogs in relation to their biological and hereditary background. The book covers all aspects of the dog as well as the difference between intelligence and association.

Campbell, William E., *Behavior Problems in Dogs.* Santa Barbara: American Veterinary Publications, 1975.

A survey of common and not-so-common behavior problems with specific instructions on how to solve them. Analyzes causes of problem behavior and suggests ways to modify the dog's behavior in his own environment. Explores in depth the influence of environmental factors on the dog's behavior.

Lorenz, Konrad Z., *Man Meets Dog.* Baltimore: Penguin Books, 1964.

Full of common sense and wit. A good guide for dog owners, especially the chapter on introducing a new animal into the household. Lorenz is considered the world's leading animal watcher and the father of ethology.

Pfaffenberger, Clarence J., *The New Knowledge of Dog Behavior.* New York: Howell Book House, 1963.

Explains the critical periods in a puppy's life and the causes of emotional blocks in adult dog behavior. Based on the research of Drs. Scott and Fuller at the Animal Behavior Division of the Roscoe B. Jackson Memorial Laboratory at Bar Harbor, Maine.

Sautter, Frederic J. and Glover, John A., *Behavior Development and Training of the Dog*. New York: Arco Publishing Company, 1978.

A thorough study of canine behavior including an analysis of the effects of genetics, critical periods, and the environment on the adult dog's behavior. Also includes the most recent research in learning and behavior including an approach to behavioral training techniques to cure behavior problems.

Scott, John Paul and Fuller, John L., *Genetics and the Social Behavior of the Dog*. Chicago: University of Chicago Press, 1965.

The central theme is the role of heredity in the development of behavior. A report on almost twenty years of research at the Roscoe B. Jackson Memorial Laboratory at Bar Harbor, Maine dealing with rearing methods, basic behavior patterns and the physiological and behavioral development of puppies.

Trumler, Eberhard, *Understanding Your Dog*. London: Faber & Faber, 1973.

Describes the dog from cradle to grave, including all aspects of their physical and behavioral development, the specific features common to all individuals of the same species, and the differences characterizing individual personalities. Succinctly explains the dog's developmental stages, not only as a puppy, but as an adult as well.

BREEDING

Harmer, Hilary, *Dogs and How to Breed Them*. London: John Gifford, Ltd., 1974.

A thorough treatment of the subject of breeding dogs from selection of breeding stock through the sale of the puppies. Includes an easy reference whelping checklist.

Seranne, Ann, *The Joy of Breeding Your Own Show Dog*. New York: Howell Book House, 1980.

A book for everyone who wants to breed a dog for whatever purpose. Contains all the advice you need from theory to practice. You will do yourself a favor to read this book before embarking upon such an important undertaking as breeding your dog.

DOG SELECTION

American Kennel Club, *The Complete Dog Book* (revised ed.). New York:

Howell Book House, 1979.

A comprehensive compendium of the breeds recognized by the American Kennel Club. Includes breed histories and breed standards as well as general information on selection and caring for your dog.

Howe, John, *Choosing the Right Dog.* New York: Harper & Row, 1976.

An honest and accurate survey of dog breeds, including the shortcomings as well as the virtues of each breed. Also contains a common sense approach to evaluating what you want in a dog.

HISTORY

Saunders, Blanche, The *Story of Dog Obedience.* New York: Howell Book House, 1974.

The story of the growth of dog training in America and how dog training got started in this country.

NUTRITION

Belfield, Wendell O. and Zucker, Martin, *How to Have a Healthier Dog.* New York: Doubleday, 1981.

The benefits of vitamins and minerals for your dog's life cycles. Provides medical and nutritional advice to enable you to set up your own preventive medicine and health program for your dog.

Collins, Donald R., *The Collins Guide to Canine Nutrition.* New York: Howell Book House, 1976.

Explains what to look for in a commercial dog food and the needs of your dog. How to evaluate different dog foods intelligently.

Levy, Juliette de Bairacli, *The Complete Herbal Book for the Dog.* New York: Arco Publishing Company, 1973.

A handbook of natural care and rearing.

Volhard, Wendy, "Back to Basics." New York: Wendy Volhard, 1980.

A guide to a balanced home-made dog food and the diet we feed our dogs.

PUPPY EVALUATION AND SELECTION

Bartlett, Melissa, "A Novice Looks at Puppy Aptitude Testing." *Pure-Bred Dogs, American Kennel Gazette,* 31-42, March, 1979.

A detailed explanation of the aptitude test compiled by Joachim and Wendy Volhard to assist a prospective puppy purchaser in the selection of a puppy suited to his family and life style. The following sources contributed to the development of this simple-to-administer test:

Campbell, William E., *Behavior Problems In Dogs.* Santa Barbara: American Veterinary Publications, 1975.

Fox, Michael W., *Understanding Your Dog.* New York: Coward, McCann, Geoghegan, 1972.

Humphrey, Elliot and Warner, Lucien, *Working Dogs.* Palo Alto: National Press, 1974.

Pfaffenberger, Clarence J., *The New Knowledge of Dog Behavior.* New York: Howell Book House, 1963.

Scott, John P. and Fuller, John L., *Genetics and the Social Behavior of the Dog.* Chicago: University of Chicago Press, 1965.

Trumler, Eberhard, *Understanding Your Dog.* London: Faber & Faber, 1973.

TRAINING

Most, Konrad, *Training Dogs.* London: Popular Dogs Publishing Company, 1954.

Most is the pioneer and father of dog training as we know it today. His manual was written in 1910 and remains the single-most important text for the serious trainer.

The Monks of New Skete, *How to Be Your Dog's Best Friend.* New York: Little, Brown & Company, 1978.

A sound and common sense approach to raising and training your dog with a wealth of insights to help you understand, appreciate and respect your dog.

INDEX

BIBLIOGRAPHY

ALL OWNERS of pure-bred dogs will benefit themselves and their dogs by enriching their knowledge of breeds and of canine care, training, breeding, psychology and other important aspects of dog management. The following list of books covers further reading recommended by judges, veterinarians, breeders, trainers and other authorities. Books may be obtained at the finer book stores and pet shops, or through Howell Book House Inc., publishers, New York.

BREED BOOKS

AFGHAN HOUND, Complete	Miller & Gilbert
AIREDALE, New Complete	Edwards
AKITA, Complete	Linderman & Funk
ALASKAN MALAMUTE, Complete	Riddle & Seeley
BASSET HOUND, New Complete	Braun
BLOODHOUND, Complete	Brey & Reed
BOXER, Complete	Denlinger
BRITTANY SPANIEL, Complete	Riddle
BULLDOG, New Complete	Hanes
BULL TERRIER, New Complete	Eberhard
CAIRN TERRIER, New Complete	Marvin
CHESAPEAKE BAY RETRIEVER, Complete	Cherry
CHIHUAHUA, Complete	Noted Authorities
COCKER SPANIEL, New	Kraeuchi
COLLIE, New	Official Publication of the Collie Club of America
DACHSHUND, The New	Meistrell
DALMATIAN, The	Treen
DOBERMAN PINSCHER, New	Walker
ENGLISH SETTER, New Complete	Tuck, Howell & Graef
ENGLISH SPRINGER SPANIEL, New	Goodall & Gasow
FOX TERRIER, New	Nedell
GERMAN SHEPHERD DOG, New Complete	Bennett
GERMAN SHORTHAIRED POINTER, New	Maxwell
GOLDEN RETRIEVER, New Complete	Fischer
GORDON SETTER, Complete	Look
GREAT DANE, New Complete	Noted Authorities
GREAT DANE, The—Dogdom's Apollo	Draper
GREAT PYRENEES, Complete	Strang & Giffin
IRISH SETTER, New Complete	Eldredge & Vanacore
IRISH WOLFHOUND, Complete	Starbuck
JACK RUSSELL TERRIER, Complete	Plummer
KEESHOND, New Complete	Cash
LABRADOR RETRIEVER, New Complete	Warwick
LHASA APSO, Complete	Herbel
MALTESE, Complete	Cutillo
MASTIFF, History and Management of the	Baxter & Hoffman
MINIATURE SCHNAUZER, New	Kiedrowski
NEWFOUNDLAND, New Complete	Chern
NORWEGIAN ELKHOUND, New Complete	Wallo
OLD ENGLISH SHEEPDOG, Complete	Mandeville
PEKINGESE, Quigley Book of	Quigley
PEMBROKE WELSH CORGI, Complete	Sargent & Harper
POODLE, New	Irick
POODLE CLIPPING AND GROOMING BOOK, Complete	Kalstone
PORTUGUESE WATER DOG, Complete	Braund & Miller
ROTTWEILER, Complete	Freeman
SAMOYED, New Complete	Ward
SCOTTISH TERRIER, New Complete	Marvin
SHETLAND SHEEPDOG, The New	Riddle
SHIH TZU, Joy of Owning	Seranne
SHIH TZU, The (English)	Dadds
SIBERIAN HUSKY, Complete	Demidoff
TERRIERS, The Book of All	Marvin
WEIMARANER, Guide to the	Burgoin
WEST HIGHLAND WHITE TERRIER, Complete	Marvin
WHIPPET, Complete	Pegram
YORKSHIRE TERRIER, Complete	Gordon & Bennett

BREEDING

ART OF BREEDING BETTER DOGS, New	Onstott
BREEDING YOUR OWN SHOW DOG	Seranne
HOW TO BREED DOGS	Whitney
HOW PUPPIES ARE BORN	Prine
INHERITANCE OF COAT COLOR IN DOGS	Little

CARE AND TRAINING

BEYOND BASIC DOG TRAINING	Bauman
COUNSELING DOG OWNERS, Evans Guide for	Evans
DOG OBEDIENCE, Complete Book of	Saunders
NOVICE, OPEN AND UTILITY COURSES	Saunders
DOG CARE AND TRAINING FOR BOYS AND GIRLS	Saunders
DOG NUTRITION, Collins Guide to	Collins
DOG TRAINING FOR KIDS	Benjamin
DOG TRAINING, Koehler Method of	Koehler
DOG TRAINING Made Easy	Tucker
GO FIND! Training Your Dog to Track	Davis
GROOMING DOGS FOR PROFIT	Gold
GUARD DOG TRAINING, Koehler Method of	Koehler
MOTHER KNOWS BEST—The Natural Way to Train Your Dog	Benjamin
OPEN OBEDIENCE FOR RING, HOME AND FIELD, Koehler Method of	Koehler
STONE GUIDE TO DOG GROOMING FOR ALL BREEDS	Stone
SUCCESSFUL DOG TRAINING, The Pearsall Guide to	Pearsall
TEACHING DOG OBEDIENCE CLASSES—Manual for Instructors	Volhard & Fisher
TOY DOGS, Kalstone Guide to Grooming All	Kalstone
TRAINING THE RETRIEVER	Kersley
TRAINING TRACKING DOGS, Koehler Method of	Koehler
TRAINING YOUR DOG—Step by Step Manual	Volhard & Fisher
TRAINING YOUR DOG TO WIN OBEDIENCE TITLES	Morsell
TRAIN YOUR OWN GUN DOG, How to	Goodall
UTILITY DOG TRAINING, Koehler Method of	Koehler
VETERINARY HANDBOOK, Dog Owner's Home	Carlson & Giffin

GENERAL

A DOG'S LIFE	Burton & Allaby
AMERICAN KENNEL CLUB 1884-1984—A Source Book	American Kennel Club
CANINE TERMINOLOGY	Spira
COMPLETE DOG BOOK, The	Official Publication of American Kennel Club
DOG IN ACTION, The	Lyon
DOG BEHAVIOR, New Knowledge of	Pfaffenberger
DOG JUDGE'S HANDBOOK	Tietjen
DOG PSYCHOLOGY	Whitney
DOGSTEPS, The New	Elliott
DOG TRICKS	Haggerty & Benjamin
EYES THAT LEAD—Story of Guide Dogs for the Blind	Tucker
FRIEND TO FRIEND—Dogs That Help Mankind	Schwartz
FROM RICHES TO BITCHES	Shattuck
HAPPY DOG/HAPPY OWNER	Siegal
IN STITCHES OVER BITCHES	Shattuck
JUNIOR SHOWMANSHIP HANDBOOK	Brown & Mason
OUR PUPPY'S BABY BOOK (blue or pink)	
SUCCESSFUL DOG SHOWING, Forsyth Guide to	Forsyth
WHY DOES YOUR DOG DO THAT?	Bergman
WILD DOGS in Life and Legend	Riddle
WORLD OF SLED DOGS, From Siberia to Sport Racing	Coppinger